A Concise Greek Grammar Workbook

A Concise Greek Grammar Workbook

Student Edition

Jamin Andreas Hübner

Hills Publishing Group • Rapid City, South Dakota

A Concise Greek Grammar Workbook
Copyright ©2018 Jamin Andreas Hübner
All Rights Reserved.
Printed in the United States of America
Student Edition

Hills Publishing Group
Rapid City, South Dakota
hillspublishinggroup@protonmail.com

ISBN-13: 978-0-9905943-5-2

Unless otherwise noted, all biblical quotations are from the *New Revised Standard Version Bible,* copyright 1989, Division of Christian Education of the Natonal Council of the Churches of Christ in the United States of America. Used by permission. All rights reserved.

All quotations marked "NASB" come from the NEW AMERICAN STANDARD BIBLE®, Copyright © 1960,1962,1963,1968,1971,1972,1973,
1975,1977,1995 by The Lockman Foundation. Used by permission.

Cover photo by Jamin Andreas Hübner, the "Madaba Map" in Madaba, Jordan (taken January 11, 2013 at Saint George Byzantine Orthodox Church)

CONTENTS

Abbreviations 6

Introduction 9

1. Alphabet and Pronunciation 18
2. First and Second Declension Nouns 28
3. Articles, Prepositions, and Third Declension Nouns 45
4. Adjectives and Adverbs 58
5. Personal Pronouns 67
6. Demonstrative and Relative Pronouns 79
7. Introduction to Verbs and Present Active Indicative 88
8. Present Middle/Passive and Contract Verbs 97
9. Imperfect and εἰμί 108
10. Future Active/Middle and Stem/Root Changes 120
11. Future Passive and Aorist 131
12. Perfect and PluPerfect 146
13. Subjunctive and Infinitive 156
14. Imperative and μι Verbs 165

ABBREVIATIONS

abbr.	abbreviation
acc.	accusative
act.	active
adj.	adjective
adv.	adverb
alt.	alternate/alternative
aor.	aorist
art.	article
BBG	*Basics of Biblical Greek* (2009)
BDAG	Bauer, Danker, Arndt, Gingrich, *A Greek-English Lexicon of the New Testament* (2000)
c.	circa, about
CEV	Century English Version
CL	*The Concise Greek-English Lexicon of the New Testament* (2009)
cog.	cognate
dat.	dative
def.	definition/definite
dem.	demonstrative
e.g.,	*exempli gratia,* for example
esp.	especially
f.	and verse following
ff.	and verses following
fem.	feminine
freq.	frequently
fut.	future
ESV	English Standard Version
gen.	genitive
GGBB	*Greek Grammar Beyond the Basics* (1998)
Heb.	Hebrew
Hübner	Hübner's translation
i.e.,	*id est*, it is, that is
IGEL	*An Intermediate Greek-English Lexicon* (1945)

ind.	indicative
indef.	indefinite
inf.	infinitive
impf.	imperfect
impv.	imperative
KJV	King James Version
LXX	Septuagint
masc.	masculine
ms.	manuscript
mss.	manuscripts
n.	noun
NA26	Nestle-Aland 26th Edition
NA27	Nestle-Aland 27th Edition
NA28	Nestle-Aland 28th Edition
NASB	New American Standard Bible (1995 ed.)
NET	New English Translation
NIV	New International Version (2011 ed.)
NLT	New Living Translation (2nd ed.)
nom.	nominative
NRSV	New Revised Standard Version
NT	New Testament
obj.	object
OT	Old Testament
pass.	passive
pf.	perfect
pl.	plural
pos.	positive
poss.	posessive
ppos.	post-positive
prep.	preposition
pres.	present
prim.	primarily
pron.	pronoun
ptc.	participle

reflex.	reflexive
RSV	Revised Standard Version
sg.	singular
subj.	subject
suff.	suffix
TNIV	Today's New International Version
trad.	traditionally
temp.	temporal
UBS	United Bible Society
UBS4	United Bible Society Greek NT, 4th Edition
UBS5	United Bible Society Greek NT, 5th Edition
v.	verse/verb
vv.	verses
w.	with

Introduction

This workbook corresponds to *A Concise Greek Grammar*. Here are a few notes and tips about using this workbook as a student:

1. Treat these workbooks as much as possible as tests. If you find yourself continually having to refer to the grammar for every single question, rehearse the grammar material more (e.g., on scratch paper) before doing this workbook.
2. Most (but not all) unknown vocabulary words in the translation portions are defined. For ones that are not defined, use a lexicon to find out what they mean.
3. For the vocabulary portions of each chapter, you must only memorize the first two renderings for each semantic category, not the entire entry as it appears in the grammar. For those of you who go above and beyond this requirement and complete the entire entry with all of its renderings for every semantic category (as it appears in the grammar), bonus points may be awarded.
4. The *Parsing Guide* and *Translation Guide* below is something you are going to refer back to continually during the first few weeks. Most of it won't make sense until beginning the actual workbook exercises. In any case, you should get familiar with these sections, and don't forget that they are here!
5. The page numbers of this workbook do *not* correspond to the page numbers of either the teacher edition workbook or the grammar.

Parsing Guide

For each portion of this workbook (except for chapter 1), you will be required to "parse" Greek words. Parsing is properly identifying every grammatical aspect of a word. Below is a list of column titles from parsing sheets and a brief summary of their possible answers:

1. "Inflected" = the word pulled out of a Greek sentence. It's the puzzle you need to solve.
2. "Case" = Nominative (Nom), Genitive (Gen), Dative (Dat), or Accusative (Acc).
3. "Number" = Singular (sg) or Plural (pl)
4. "Gender" = Masculine (M), Feminine (F), or Neuter (N).
5. "Person" = 1st, 2nd, or 3rd.
6. "Tense" = Present (Pres), Imperfect (Imp), Future (Fut), Aorist (Aor), Perfect (Perf), or Pluperfect (Plu)
7. "Voice" = Active (Act), Middle (Mid), Middle/Passive (M/P), Deponent (Dep), or Passive (Pas).
8. "Mood" = Indicative (Ind), Subjunctive (Sub), Imperative (Imp), or Optative (Opt).
9. "Lexical Form" = the term as it appears in a lexicon.
10. "Gloss" = your translation of the inflected word.

Parsing Tips

1. You must have the entirety of the vocabulary entry in the lexical form (e.g., for nouns, you must have the genitive singular ending and the article in addition to the word).
2. You should remember that many nouns can have multiple possibilities (e.g., can be M/F/N gender, or can be Nom *or* Acc Pl), and verbs can have multiple possibilities (e.g., e[labon can be either 1st Sg or 3rd Pl). *You must include both possibilities to receive full credit.*
3. You are required to translate dative and gentive nouns with their keywords ("to"/ "in"/ "with," and "of") when filling out the "inflected meaning" section. If you do not include these keywords, they will be counted as wrong.
4. When parsing prepositions, you must include all the possible cases of their antecendent (e.g., παρά should have "Gen/Dat/Acc" under the Case column, and nothing under the Gender and Number columns).

5. Deponent verbs should (in present and imperfect tenses) have "Dep" in the "voice" column, while verbs having middle/passive endings should have "Mid," "Pas," or "Mid/Pas" under the "Voice" column.

6. How do you know when the voice is either "Mid," "Pas," or "Mid/Pas"? The answer is found in the *Table of Verb Tenses*. If the verb tense you are dealing with has "mid/pas" under the "tense" column in the *Table of Verb Tenses*, for example, then he/she must put "mid/pas" under the "voice" column while parsing. Follow the same rule for active and passive verbs. (Notice that only imperfect, present, and perfect tense verbs have "mid/pas" on the *Table of Verb Tenses*—and that's because these tenses have the same form when being either middle or passive voice.)

7. You are not required to know which aorist form is used; "Aor" is sufficient when encountering First, Second, and Liquid Aorists.

Tips on Study and Translation

There are two maxims that I drill into my students from day one:

"A little bit of Greek is dangerous."

"Translation is Treason."

The purpose of the first statement is to highlight the fact that NT Greek is highly abused. There are countless authors, pastors, and self-proclaimed "scholars" who have taken one or two semesters of Greek and have used it for every purpose imaginable—including purposes detrimental to the church and to the ongoing progress of biblical study. Train a teenager to load and fire a gun, and you've created a dangerous situation. But train that same teenager how to clean and maintain it, teach him/her what kind of gun and cartridge is appropriate for certain situations, when and why it is appropriate to fire, how to hold it when firing, how to control breathing when firing, and how to safely store it when not firing, then, after practice and many trips to the firing range, you may eventually have trained a true marksman or markswoman.

The same is true for Greek. I *highly* recommend students to take second-year Greek. As difficult as it is to commit two years of life to learning a language, it is preferable if the students' goal is long-term engagement with the world of Jesus and the teachings of the NT. Our goal is not to impress friends or our congregations, nor simply to gain enough knowledge to refute theological ideas we don't like. Our goal is to enter into the world of the text and, by the "illumination of the Spirit," be transformed by it.

The purpose of the second statement ("translation is treason") is to underscore the nature of all translation. The phrase, "no Bible translation is perfect" is often heard. But few actually understand what this means. Many understand this to mean that, "people are fallible, so they always make mistakes," as if a sinless team of scholars would be able to produce a perfect translation of the Bible. But this is not the case.

The truth is that no translation is perfect because, in addition to the fallibility of persons, no two languages are interchangeable. The nature of translation requires that *information (or "semantic content") be lost* in the process of moving from one language to another. There are three genders and over a dozen verb tenses in Greek. English has no grammatical gender and less than a dozen verb tenses. Pure conversion in this sense is impossible. Nuances and meaning are often lost in translation not simply because the translation is "bad," "liberal," "conservative," "cultic," or what have you, but just because that is the nature of translation.

Translation is also "treason" because it often *requires* interpretation. One of the most popular attitudes about translation is that the "best" translation is one that is word-for-word literal because this circumvents the bias of translators. This is partially, but not entirely true. All translators must engage in interpretation, regardless of how they decide to translate. For example, the Greek term gunhv means either "woman" or "wife." Context determines whether it is one or the other. Since English has two different words for these two different meanings (a female person or a female person who is married), the translator *must* make a choice between the two. (It must also be decided which will be in the primary text and which will be relegated to a footnote/marginal note.) This requires interpretation, and the answers are not always clear.[1]

This is one reason why *multiple Bible translations are necessary*. Some translations try to translate the Greek text literally, "word-for-word" (usually called "formal" translations). This is often beneficial for retaining certain ordering of phrases, words, and even meanings. But, it also creates problems beyond those already mentioned above. It takes up to four, even five English words to translate a single Greek word. Furthermore, some Greek words aren't even translatable at all (such as ἄν, making a statement contingent).

Other translations proceed on a more "thought-for-thought" basis (usually called "dynamic-equivalent" or "functionally-equivalent" translations).[2] This gives translators the freedom to use

---

[1] For an engaging study of this particular problem, see the discussion of 1 Timothy 3:11 in Jamin Hübner, *A Case for Female Deacons* (Eugene: Wipf and Stock, 2015).

[2] "Dynamic equivalence" was coined by Eugene Nida in the 1960s. Nida and J. P. Louw authored the excellent reference work *Greek-English Lexicon of the New Testament: Based on Semantic Domains* (New York: United Bible Societies: 1999).

the vocabulary necessary to communicate what the author was intending to communicate. But this also introduces its own set of problems, such as amplifying translational bias in interpretation, misleading readers about what words or phrases come first in a sentence, etc. Paraphrase and other translations oriented at capturing idioms face the same problem. So for every advantage, there is at least one disadvantage.

All of this means that multiple translations *of different kinds* are necessary for effective study. This introduces another important topic: the effective use of different translations.

The Translation Triangle

"What is the best English translation?"

Every professor of Greek gets hammered with this question countless times. And there are many popular answers to it:

1. "Here, this translation is the best. There you go."
2. "Just get all kinds of translations and compare them, and choose whatever one makes sense to you."
3. "Oh, don't bother, it doesn't matter what translation you have, they will all tell you essentially the same thing."

While these kinds of answers are common, they are littered with problems. Recommendation 1 is erroneous because no single translation is absolutely sufficient for deep study (refer to "Tips on Study and Translation" above). Recommendation 2 is erroneous because not all translations are of equal value. Recommendation 3 is misleading because the accuracy of the translation determines how close one is to the earliest text(s) of scripture.

Clearly, some discernment is required. One should have *several good* translations, translations of different *kinds*, and one should give more *weight* to some translations over others. How can all of these three major concerns be effectively addressed without confusing the average student?

Over the years of teaching, research, preaching, and publishing, I've landed on three "favorites" that fit the ticket for efficiency: the NRSV, NIV, and CEB. This "translation triangle" assists in selecting, prioritizing, and utilizing some of the best English translations available as they translate and study the scriptures.

New Revised Standard Version (NRSV)
- *Formal Equivalency*
- "Word-for-word"
- Produced mostly by both Christian and secular university scholars

Common English Bible (CEB)
- *Dynamic-Paraphrase*
- "Idiomatically powerful"
- Produced mainly by Christian seminary professors

New International Version (NIV)
- *Dynamic (Functional) Equivalency*
- "Thought-for-thought"
- Produced by a mix of Christian university scholars and seminary professors

A couple brief comments are in order.

First, as noted above, my choice of these three versions comes from years of study regarding the nature of translation, "weeding out" those that are largely inferior (e.g., in textual criticism, quality of scholarship, consistency in methodology, undue or exaggerated bias, methods and resources utilized in the translation teams, etc.). Most translations aren't just inferior but unnecessary. They exist for no other reason than for profiting Christian publishers by strategically avoiding the royalty fees associated with other translations.[3]

In any case, these three are not alone in being "good translations," but they (1) exhibit the full range of translation philosophies; (2) are produced by a massive team of qualified scholars; (3) are widely recognized and used. So, while I will not spend pages defending my choices (which are subjective), I will simply say that they aren't arbitrary.

---

[3] Crossway owns the rights to the ESV; Zondervan owns the rights to the NIV; Thomas Nelson owns the rights to the NKJV; B&H the CSB, etc.). In other words, publishers save money by producing, printing, and distributing their own legally-owned translation, and that is how many modern translations originate in the first place.

In using the "triangle," the basic rule is *students should begin with the NRSV (literal) and work their way around to the CEB (idiomatic) as they study.* Literal translations are just that—literal. They provide the raw materials for Bible study—the closest reflection of Greek words and structure in English sentences. They do not, however, attempt to provide considerable interpretational insight. How can one gauge if an interpretation is possible and/or plausible? The answer is simple: move on to the next translation for more guidance.

Whatever the situation may be, and despite its limitations, I have found the Triangle immensely effective in helping students of scripture efficiently and accurately study the Bible and get a grip on the "translation wars." Hopefully you will to!

Translation Guide

For each portion of this workbook, students will be required to translate Greek texts into English. This can be a daunting task at first. But the whole process is easier if students follow five basic steps: (1) Identify and Translate Familiar Words; (2) Identify Subject and Predicate; (3) Write Out Initial Translation; (4) Write Out Remaining Translation; (5) Compare Translations:

1. Identify the words that you know, and write in the gloss (English translation) right above each word. Use a lexicon to look up words that you don't know.

> and/but   to/with   him   every/all   Judea
> καὶ ἐξεπορεύετο (going out) πρὸς αὐτὸν πᾶσα ἡ Ἰουδαία
> ?   and/but   Jerusalem   every/all   and/but
> χώρα καὶ οἱ Ἱεροσολυμῖται πάντες, καὶ ἐβαπτίζοντο (were
>   by   of him   in/on   Jordan
> being baptized) ὑπ' αὐτοῦ ἐν τῷ Ἰορδάνῃ ποταμῷ (river)
>   sins   of them/their
> ἐξομολογούμενοι (confessing) τὰς ἁμαρτίας αὐτῶν.

2. Identify the subject (nominative nouns) and predicate (verbs), and start thinking about how to pair them up in an English phrase. Include any matching adjectives and modifiers.

[Diagrammed Greek text with annotations:]

καὶ ἐξεπορεύετο (going out) πρὸς αὐτὸν πᾶσα ἡ Ἰουδαία χώρα καὶ οἱ Ἱεροσολυμῖται πάντες, καὶ ἐβαπτίζοντο (were being baptized) ὑπ' αὐτοῦ ἐν τῷ Ἰορδάνῃ ποταμῷ (river) ἐξομολογούμενοι (confessing) τὰς ἁμαρτίας αὐτῶν.

3. Write out the first portion of the Greek sentence in English as best as you can.

And all the country of Judea and all Jerusalem were going out to him,

4. Repeat these steps for the next portion of the Greek text.

And all the country of Judea and all Jerusalem were going out to him, and were being baptized by him in the Jordan river confessing their sins.

5. Compare your final translation with other English translations, using the *Translation Triangle*. Note any differences, and consider whether they reflect the Greek text or not:
   - NRSV: "And people from the whole Judean countryside and all the people of Jerusalem were going out to him, and were baptized by him in the river Jordan, confessing their sins."
   - NIV: "The whole Judean countryside and all the people of Jerusalem went out to him. Confessing their sins, they were baptized by him in the Jordan River."
   - CEB: "People from Jerusalem, throughout Judea, and all around the Jordan River came to him. As they confessed their sins, he baptized them in the Jordan River."

1

Alphabet, Pronunciation, and Punctuation

1.1 Alphabet

α α α α _____

β _____

γ _____

δ _____

ε _____

ζ _____

η _____

ϑ (one-stroke) _____

θ (two-stroke) _____

ι _____

ϰ (one-stroke) _____

κ (two-stroke) _____

λ _____

μ _____

ν _____

ξ _____

ο _____

π _____

ρ _____

σ/ς _____

τ _____

υ _____

φ (one-stroke) _____

ϕ (two-stroke) _____

χ _____

ψ _____

ω _____

Α _A_ _A_____

Β _____

Γ _____

Δ _____

Ε _____

Ζ _____

Η _____

Θ _____

Ι _____

Κ _____

Λ _____

Μ _____

Ν _____

Ξ _____

Ο _____

Π _____

Ρ _____

Σ _____

Τ _____

Υ _____

Φ _____

Χ _____

Ψ _____

Ω _____

1. Fill-in the blank:

Name	Capital	Small	Examples	Name in Greek
			Alm or apple	
			Victory	
			yellow/goat	
			those	
			Energy	
			Zebra/suds	
			Café	
			Thumb	
			Fin/Ski	
			Kids	
			Link	
			Monkey	
			Name	
			Axiom	
			Open	
			Popcorn	
			Rule	
			Student	
			Tutor	
			Skew (über)	
			Photon	
			Loch	
			Tips	
			Cone	

2. What are the two kinds of sigmas and when are they used?
   _____

3. What is the number for ιδ´? ____

4. What is the number for ρδ´? ____

5. What is the number for ͵βγγ? _____

1.2 Consonants

1. Most people who learn New Testament Greek today properly pronounce it (that is, pronounce it like it was spoken during the first-century).
   True or False

2. What is the difference between a stop and a fricative consonant?
   _____

3. Fill-in the *Table of Stops and Fricatives*:

   | | Stops | Fricatives | |
		Hard	Soft
Labial			
Velar			
Dental			

4. If a is σ added to a κ, what letter is formed? ___

5. When are gammas pronounced like a "g" sound ("grass")?
   _____

6. What is a *gamma nasal*?
   _____

7. When are zetas pronounced like an English z?
   _____

1.3 Vowels and Diphthongs

1. What are the Greek vowels? _____

2. If an iota is the first letter of a word, how is it pronounced?
   _____

3. ε and o at the end of words are often replaced by what two vowels? _____ _____

4. Define the following:

   a. *Improper Diphthong*: _____

   b. *Dieresis*: _____
   _____

   c. *Diphthong*: _____

   d. *Iota subscript*: _____

5. Fill-in the *Table of Greek Diphthongs*:

Diphthong	Eng. Examples
	B<u>et</u>
	Rec<u>ei</u>ve
	D<u>ew</u>
	S<u>ui</u>te
	<u>A</u>fter/<u>a</u>venue
	Gr<u>ou</u>p
	Eff<u>e</u>ct/<u>e</u>very

1.4 Accents

1. What is the primary function of accents?
   _____

2. List and define the three positions of accents:

   a. _____: _____

   b. _____: _____

   c. _____: _____

3. What accent only falls on an ultima? _____

4. What accent never falls on an ultima? _____

5. Accents never change; they always remain in the same positions for each given word. True or False
6. Grave accents change to acute accents if they are not followed by another Greek word. True or False
7. Circumflex accents do not affect pronunciation. True or False

1.5 Breathing Marks

1. Rough breathing marks do not change pronunciation. True or False
2. Rhos at the beginning of words always have a rough breathing mark. True or False
3. Where are breathing marks placed in the case of diphthongs?

_____

1.6 Punctuation

1. Translate:

   Ἰησοῦ Χριστοῦ; = _____

   Ἰησοῦ Χριστοῦ· = _____

2. Greek does not distinguish between colons and semicolons. True or False
3. Greek has no quotation marks. True or False
4. In Greek, the first letter of a paragraph is capitalized. True or False

1.8 Vocabulary

1. Vocabulary entries consist of three parts:
   a. The word, always in the _____ _____ case, or "lexical form."
   b. The _____ ____ _____.
   c. The_____.
2. Students are required to memorize what of the vocabulary entries?
   a. The entire entry
   b. Only the first definition
   c. The first two renderings of each semantic category
   d. Any random three words from the definition

Vocabulary

Ἀβραάμ, ὁ
ἄγγελος, -ου, ὁ
ἀμήν
ἄνθρωπος, -ου, ὁ
ἀπόστολος, -ου, ὁ
Γαλιλαία, -ας, ἡ
γραφή, -ῆς, ἡ
Δαυίδ, ὁ
δόξα, -ης, ἡ
ἐγώ
ἔσχατος, -η, ον
ζωή, -ῆς, ἡ
θεός, -οῦ, ὁ
καί
καρδία, -ας, ἡ
κόσμος, -ου, ὁ
λόγος, -ου, ὁ
Παῦλος, -ου, ὁ
Πέτρος, -ου, ὁ
Πιλᾶτος, -ου, ὁ
πνεῦμα, -ατος, τό
προφήτης, -ου, ὁ
σάββατον, -ου, τό
Σίμων, ωνος, ὁ
φωνή, -ῆς, ἡ
Χριστός, -ου, ὁ

_____	Abraham
_____	1) and; 2) also, even
_____	a) messenger, delegate; b) ambassador, apostle, envoy
_____	1) the Anointed one, Messiah, Christ; 2) Christ
_____	David
_____	Galilee
_____	glory, honor
_____	God, god
_____	1) heart; 2) heart, interior, center
_____	I
_____	last; a) the end; d) least, most insignificant
_____	life
_____	a human being, person, someone, somebody
_____	messenger, envoy, attendant (trad. *angel*)
_____	Paul
_____	Peter
_____	Pilate
_____	1-2) prophet
_____	1) Sabbath; 2) week
_____	Simon
_____	1) sound, noise; 2) voice, tone; 3) language
_____	1) wind, breath, spirit; (3) spirit, apparition, ghost; 4) spirit, holy spirit
_____	amen (so let it be)
_____	1) word, statement, message, speech; 2) word, reason
_____	1) adornment; 2) universe, world; 3-4) world
_____	scripture

2

First and Second Declension Nouns

2.1 General Morphology

1. The smallest grammatical unit of language is a _____.
2. What is the difference between a freestanding morpheme and a bound morpheme?
   _____
3. Nouns, adjectives, and verbs never share the same roots. True or False
4. Bound morphemes can be prefixes or suffixes. True or False
5. A stem is _____
6. Declension and conjugation are both cases of inflection; one applies to nouns and the other applies to verbs. True or False
7. Indeclinable words are nouns that _____.
8. What might a "gloss" refer to?
   a. _____
   b. _____
   c. _____
9. What are "lemma"?

10. There is basically no difference between a "dictionary" and "lexicon." True or False

2.2 Morphology of Greek Nouns

1. A word or group of words that function as a noun is called a _____.
2. Case endings are _____.
3. Greek nouns have _____ (how many?) major case endings:
    a. _____ case, where the noun functions as the subject.
    b. _____ case, where the noun modifies another noun.
    c. _____ case, where the noun functions as the indirect object.
    d. _____ case, where the noun functions as the direct object.
4. In the following English sentence, please identify the basic function (subj., v., dir. obj., indir. obj., or adj.) of the words:
    a. "After supper, I wrote a large letter to my sister."
        i. I: _____
        ii. wrote: _____
        iii. large: _____
        iv. letter: _____
        v. to…sister: _____
    b. "For two years in the international space station, Professor Hübner taught Koiné Greek."
        i. international: _____
        ii. space station: _____
        iii. Greek: _____
        iv. Professor Hübner: _____

v. Taught: _____

vi. Koiné: _____

5. Fill-in the *Table of Case Endings*:

	2ⁿᵈ	1ˢᵗ	2ⁿᵈ	3ʳᵈ	
	Masc	**Fem**	**Neut**	M/F	Neut
Sg Nom				ς / -	-
Sg Gen				ος	ος
Sg Dat				ι	ι
Sg Acc				α / ν	-
Pl Nom				ες	α
Pl Gen				ων	ων
Pl Dat				σι(ν)	σι(ν)
Pl Acc				ας	α

6. Greek usually uses a singular verb when the subject is neuter plural. True or False

7. The iota case endings of all dative singular nouns subscript. True or False

8. Match each case with the appropriate declined, underlined words:
   a. Nominative Case   ___. ἐν νόμῳ <u>τοῦ θεοῦ</u>
   b. Accusative Case   ___. καὶ <u>θεὸς</u> ἦν ὁ λόγος
   c. Dative Case   ___. καὶ ὁ λόγος ἦν πρὸς <u>τὸν θεόν</u>
   d. Genitive Case   ___. Μακάριοι οἱ πτωχοὶ <u>τῷ πνεύματι</u>

2.3 Grammatical Gender

1. The (grammatical) gender of some words change. True or False
2. An easy way to tell the gender of a word is to look at what article it has in a lexicon. True or False
3. Identify the gender of the following words:
   a. Βασιλεία, -ας, -ἡ _____
   b. καιρός, -ου, ὁ _____
   c. Εὐαγγέλιον, -ου, τό _____
   d. ἀρχή, -ῆς, ἡ _____
   e. ἔργον, -ου, τό _____
   f. ἐξουσία, -ας, ἡ _____
   g. κύριος, -ου, ὁ _____

2.4 Declension

1. Greek cases are divided up by grammatical gender into three _____. The **Three** _____ _____ are:
   a. _____
   b. _____
   c. _____

2.5 The Four Rules of First and Second Declension Nouns

1. _____
2. _____
3. _____
4. _____

2.6-2.9 The Greek Cases in Detail

1. Match the following nominatives with the English phrases:

    a. "My Father is <u>the professor</u>."   __. Subject Nominative
    b. "<u>Jill</u> climbed the tree."   __. Predicate Nominative
    c. "Gilbert the <u>lucky boy</u> won the lottery." __. Appositional Nominative

2. Match the following genitives with the English phrases:

    a. "A third <u>of the pie</u> is gone."   __. Relational Genitive
    b. "That coat <u>of his</u> has dirt on it."   __. Definitional Genit.
    c. "Susan <u>of the Johnsons</u> is coming over."   __. Possessive Genitive
    d. "You will receive the gift <u>of the Holy Spirit</u>."   __. Objective Genitive
    e. "Enemies <u>of faith</u>…" ("Enemies <u>against faith</u>…") __. Partitive Genitive
    f. "Her room <u>of disgust</u>…" ("Her <u>disgusting</u> room") __. Attributed Genitive
    g. "The newness <u>of life</u>…" ("The new <u>life</u>")   __. Attributive Genit.
    h. "Students <u>of mischief</u> shall die."   __. Descriptive Genit.

3. Match the following datives with the English phrases:

    a. "Navy Seals shoot <u>with accuracy</u>."   __. Instrumental Dat.
    b. "Who are the people traveling <u>with her</u>?"   __. Causal Dative
    c. "He translated the Bible <u>by hard work</u>."   __. Adverbial Dative
    d. "The argument failed <u>because of poor logic</u>." __. Associate Dative

4. Match the following accusatives with the English phrases:

    a. "Go get <u>him</u> some <u>food</u>."   __. Direct Obj. Acc
    b. "Adding honey makes <u>everything</u> taste good." __. Object-Compl Acc.
    c. "Consider <u>it done</u>."   __. Infinitive Subj Acc
    d. "He slammed the <u>car door</u> to vent his anger." __. Appositional Acc.
    e. "Believe in the Lord <u>Jesus</u>."   __. Person-Thing Acc

Identifying Nominative Nouns

Please circle, underline, or highlight the appropriate Greek and English word for each case ending (all words are vocabulary words that you know).

Nominative Masculine

καὶ ὁ οὐρανὸς ὑετὸν ἔδωκεν καὶ ἡ γῆ ἐβλάστησεν τὸν καρπὸν αὐτῆς.
And heaven gave rain and the earth yielded its harvest. (Js 5:18)

καὶ ὁ οὐρανὸς ἀπεχωρίσθη ὡς βιβλίον ἑλισσόμενον
The sky vanished like a scroll rolling itself up. (Rev 6:14)

Οἱ οὐρανοὶ διηγοῦνται δόξαν θεοῦ
The skies above proclaims his glory. (Ps 19:1, LXX)

ὅτε δὲ ἤγγισεν ὁ καιρὸς τῶν καρπῶν
When the harvest time had come, (Mt 21:34)

τοῦτο δέ φημι, ἀδελφοί, ὁ καιρὸς συνεσταλμένος ἐστίν
I mean, brothers and sisters, the appointed time has grown short. (1 Cor 7:29)

Nominative Neuter

εἰ δὲ καὶ ἔστιν κεκαλυμμένον τὸ εὐαγγέλιον ἡμῶν
And even if our gospel is veiled, (2 Cor 4:3)

ὅτι τὸ εὐαγγέλιον ἡμῶν οὐκ ἐγενήθη εἰς ὑμᾶς ἐν λόγῳ μόνον
because our message of the gospel came not in word only, (1 Th 1:5)

ἑκάστου τὸ ἔργον φανερὸν γενήσεται
...[will] test what sort of work each has done. (1 Cor 3:13)

Nominative Feminine

Ὁ δὲ καρπὸς τοῦ πνεύματός ἐστιν ἀγάπη
By contrast, the fruit of the Spirit is love. (Gal 5:22)

ὅτι ὁ θεὸς ἀγάπη ἐστίν
...for God is love. (1 Jn 4:8)[4]

Ἐδόθη μοι πᾶσα ἐξουσία ἐν οὐρανῷ καὶ ἐπὶ τῆσ γῆς
All authority in heaven and on earth has been given to me. (Mt 28:18)

Identifying Genitives

Genitive Masculine

καὶ οἱ ἀστέρες τοῦ οὐρανοῦ ἔπεσαν εἰς τὴν γῆν
and the stars of the sky fell to the earth. (Rev 6:13)

καὶ ἰδοὺ φωνὴ ἐκ τῶν οὐρανῶν λέγουσα
And a voice from heaven said... (Mt 3:17)

Μετανοεῖτε, ἤγγικεν γὰρ ἡ βασιλεία τῶν οὐρανῶν.
Repent, for the kingdom of heaven has come near. (Mt 3:2)

Λογίζομαι γὰρ ὅτι οὐκ ἄξια τὰ παθήματα τοῦ νῦν καιροῦ πρὸς τὴν μέλλουσαν
    δόξαν ἀποκαλυφθῆναι εἰς ἡμᾶς.
I consider that the sufferings of this present time are not worth comparing with the glory about to be revealed to us. (Rom 8:18)

τὰ δὲ σημεῖα τῶν καιρῶν οὐ δύνασθε;
...but you cannot interpret the signs of the times. (Mt 16:3b)

---

[4] This is a "predicate nominative" at work.

Genitive Neuter

Ἀρχὴ τοῦ εὐαγγελίου Ἰησοῦ Χριστοῦ υἱοῦ θεοῦ
The beginning of the good news of Jesus Christ, the Son of God. (Mk 1:1)

ἀκοῦσαι τὰ ἔθνη τὸν λόγον τοῦ εὐαγγελίου καὶ πιστεῦσαι
"…the Gentiles would hear the message of the good news and become believers." (Acts 15:7)

ῥύσεταί με ὁ κύριος ἀπὸ παντὸς ἔργου πονηροῦ
The Lord will rescue me from every evil attack… (2 Tm 4:18a)

Genitive Feminine

καὶ ὁ θεὸς τῆς ἀγάπης καὶ εἰρήνης ἔσται μεθ' ὑμῶν.
And the God of love and peace will be with you. (2 Cor 13:11b)

οἱ μὲν ἐξ ἀγάπης
…these out of love. (Ph 1:16a)

καὶ κυριεύσει κυριείαν πολλὴν ἐπ' ἐξουσίας αὐτοῦ.
…and shall rule a realm greater than his own realm. (Dan 11:5, LXX)

Identifying Datives

Dative Masculine

ὅτι ἐν αὐτῷ ἐκτίσθη τὰ πάντα ἐν τοῖς οὐρανοῖς καὶ ἐπὶ τῆς γῆς
for in him all thingsin heaven and on earth were created. (Col 1:16)

χαίρετε καὶ ἀγαλλιᾶσθε, ὅτι ὁ μισθὸς ὑμῶν πολὺς ἐν τοῖς οὐρανοῖς
Rejoice and be glad, for your reward is great in heaven(s) (Mt 5:12)

καὶ αἱ δυνάμεις αἱ ἐν τοῖς οὐρανοῖς σαλευθήσονται.
...and the powers in the heavens will be shaken. (Mk 13:25)

Ἐν ἐκείνῳ τῷ καιρῷ ἀποκριθεὶς ὁ Ἰησοῦς εἶπεν
At that time Jesus said. (Mt 11:25)

ἀποκαλυφθῆναι ἐν καιρῷ ἐσχάτῳ.
to be revealed in the last time (1 Pt 1:5)

Dative Neuter

Ἀλλ' οὐ πάντες ὑπήκουσαν τῷ εὐαγγελίῳ
But not all have obeyed the good news. (Rom 10:16)

ὃς ἐγένετο ἀνὴρ προφήτης δυνατὸς ἐν ἔργῳ καὶ λόγῳ ἐναντίον τοῦ θεοῦ καὶ παντὸς τοῦ λαοῦ,
...who was a prophet mighty in deed and word before God and all the people, (Lk 24:19)

κατειργάσατο Χριστὸς δι' ἐμοῦ εἰς ὑπακοὴν ἐθνῶν, λόγῳ καὶ ἔργῳ
...what Christ has accomplished through me to win obedience from the Gentiles, by word and deed (Rom 15:18)

Dative Feminine

πάντα ὑμῶν ἐν ἀγάπῃ γινέσθω
Let all that you do be done in love. (1 Cor 16:14).

τί θέλετε; ἐν ῥάβδῳ ἔλθω πρὸς ὑμᾶς, ἢ ἐν ἀγάπῃ πνεύματί τε πραΰτητοσ
What do you prefer? Am I to come to you with a stick, or with love in a spirit of gentleness? (1 Cor 4:21)

Ἐν ποίᾳ ἐξουσίᾳ ταῦτα ποιεῖσ; καὶ τίς σοι ἔδωκεν τὴν ἐξουσίαν ταύτην
"By what authority are you doing these things, and who gave you this authority?" (Mt 21:23)

Identifying Accusatives

Accusative Masculine

οὗτοι ἔχουσιν τὴν ἐξουσίαν κλεῖσαι τὸν οὐρανόν
They have the authority to shut the sky. (Rev 11:6)

καὶ Ἰησοῦ βαπτισθέντος καὶ προσευχομένου ἀνεῳχθῆναι τὸν οὐρανὸν
…and when Jesus also had been baptized and was praying, the heaven was opened. (Lk 3:21)

ἔτι γὰρ Χριστὸς ὄντων ἡμῶν ἀσθενῶν ἔτι κατὰ καιρὸν ὑπὲρ ἀσεβῶν ἀπέθανεν
For while we were still weak, at the right time Christ died for the ungodly. (Rom 5:6)

Οὐχ ὑμῶν ἐστιν γνῶναι χρόνους ἢ καιροὺς οὓς ὁ πατὴρ ἔθετο ἐν τῇ ἰδίᾳ ἐξουσίᾳ·
It is not for you to know times or periods that the Father has set by his own authority. (Acts 1:7)

Accusative Neuter

καὶ κηρυχθήσεται τοῦτο τὸ εὐαγγέλιον τῆς βασιλείας
And this good news of the kingdom will be proclaimed… (Mt 24:14)

ἦλθεν ὁ Ἰησοῦς εἰς τὴν Γαλιλαίαν κηρύσσων τὸ εὐαγγέλιον τοῦ θεοῦ
…Jesus came to Galilee, proclaiming the good news of God, (Mk 1:14)

ἑκάστῳ τὸ ἔργον αὐτοῦ
…each with his work (Mk 13:34)

καὶ μὴ συνελθόντα αὐτοῖς εἰς τὸ ἔργον μὴ συμπαραλαμβάνειν τοῦτον

and had not accompanied them in the work. (Acts 15:38)

Accusative Feminine

ἐν δὲ τῇ εὐσεβείᾳ τὴν φιλαδελφίαν, ἐν δὲ τῇ φιλαδελφίᾳ τὴν ἀγάπην
and godliness with mutual affection, and mutual affection with love. (2 Pt 1:7)

καὶ ἦσαν ἐναντίον αὐτοῦ ὡς ἡμέραι ὀλίγαι παρὰ τὸ ἀγαπᾶν αὐτὸν αὐτήν.
and they seemed to him but a few days because of the love he had for her. (Gen 29:20, LXX)

ἦν γὰρ διδάσκων αὐτοὺς ὡς ἐξουσίαν ἔχων καὶ οὐχ ὡς οἱ γραμματεῖς αὐτῶν
…for he taught them as one who had authority, and not as their scribes. (Mt 7:29)

Vocabulary

ἀγάπη, -ης, ἡ
ἄλλος, -η, -ο
αὐτός, -ή, -ό
βασιλεία, -ας, ἡ
δέ
εἰμί
ἐν
ἔργον, -ου, τό
ἐστίν
ἦν
καιρός, -οῦ, ὁ
νῦν
ὁ, ἡ, τό
ὅτι
οὐ, οὐκ, οὐχ
ὥρα, -ας, ἡ
ἁμαρτία, -ας, ἡ
ἀρχή, -ῆς, ἡ
γάρ
εἰ
εἶπεν
εἰς
εἰσίν
ἐξουσία, -ας, ἡ
εὐαγγέλιον, -ου, τό
Ἰησοῦς, -οῦ, ὁ
κύριος, -ου, ὁ
μή
οὐρανός, -ου, ὁ
οὗτος

σύ _____
υἱός, -οῦ, ὁ _____
ὥστε _____

_____ 1) time; 2) time, period
_____ 1) now, just now; 2) as the matter now stands, now, but now, but as it is, as a matter of fact
_____ 1) authority, right, jurisdiction, privilege; 2) authority
_____ 1) beginning, start; 2) ruler, authority; 3) position, domain, jurisdiction
_____ ppos. in turn, now, so, then, and, but
_____ prep. w. dat. 1) in, on, at, among, by; 2) in; 3) with, along with, with the help of, through; 5) because of, on account of; 6) in, while, when
_____ ppos. for, then
_____ good news
_____ he/she/it is (3rd pers. sg. εἰμί)
_____ he/she/it said (3rd pers. sg. aor. λέγω)
_____ 1) heaven, sky; 2) heaven; 3) God
_____ 1) hour, time, (a/the) time; 2) time
_____ am, are, is, was, were, will be
_____ 1) into, to, toward, for, with a view to, against, about, in reference to, at, in, via, by, up to, on; 2) to, until
_____ Jesus, Joshua
_____ 1) kingship, royal power/rule/reign, royal jurisdiction, reign; 2) kingdom
_____ 1) owner, lord, master; 2) lord, master, sir
_____ 1) affection, esteem, love; 2) love feast
_____ a) no; b-c) not

	not; a) not, that...not, lest, so that...not; b) not...not *x*; c) not, not ever
_____	other
_____	he/she/it was (3rd pers. sg. impf. εἰμί)
_____	1) sin; 2) sinfulness
_____	1) self, even, very; 2) pron. he, she, it (pl. they, them); 3) same
_____	1) dem. pron. sg. this, he/she/it/they, pl. these, sg. this fellow; 2) adj. this
_____	son, descendant
_____	1) dem. pron. (namely) that; 3) ""; 4) because, for, that, inasmuch, why?
_____	1) dem. pron. this one, that one; 2) art. the
_____	1) for this reason, therefore, (and) so; 2) so that, for the purpose of, with a view to, in order that
_____	they are (pl. εἰμί)
_____	1) task, assignment; 2) deed, action; 3) a work, product; 4) thing, matter
_____	2nd pers. pron. you., you (persons), your
_____	you are (2nd pers. sg. εἰμί)

Parsing

(Refer back to the "Parsing Guide" in the introduction for help!)

	Inflected	*Case*	*Number*	*Gender*	*Lexical Form*	*Gloss*
1.	ἄνθρωπον					
2.	ὧραι					
3.	τήν					
4.	βασιλείας					
5.	θεοί					
6.	λόγους					
7.	καιροί					
8.	τάς					
9.	Χριστόν					
10.	κόσμου					
11.	δόξας					

Translation

1. ἀποστέλλω (I send) τὸν ἄγγελόν.[5] _____
2. ὅτι αὐτοὶ (they) τὸν θεὸν ὄψονται (will see).[6] _____
3. Διώκετε (Pursue) τὴν ἀγάπην.[7] _____
4. ἐραυνᾶτε (you search) τὰς γραφάς.[8] _____
5. Πεπλήρωται (he/she/it has come) ὁ καιρὸς καὶ ἤγγικεν (has drawn near) ἡ βασιλεία τοῦ θεοῦ·[9] _____
6. ἐτέλεσεν (he/she/it finished) ὁ Ἰησοῦς τοὺς λόγους.[10] _____
7. Τὸ σάββατον διὰ τὸν ἄνθρωπον ἐγένετο (he/she/it was made) καὶ οὐχ ὁ ἄνθρωπος διὰ τὸ σάββατον·[11] _____
8. καὶ ἀπέστειλεν (he/she/it sent) αὐτοὺς κηρύσσειν (to preach) τὴν βασιλείαν τοῦ θεοῦ.[12] _____
9. καὶ νῦν ἡ βασιλεία σου (your) οὐ στήσεται (he/she/it will continue).[13] _____

---

[5] Mk 1:2.
[6] Mt 5:8.
[7] 1 Cor 14:1.
[8] Jn 5:39.
[9] Mk 1:15.
[10] Mt 7:28.
[11] Mk 2:27.
[12] Lk 9:2.
[13] 1 Sam 13:14, LXX.

Review of Chapter 1

Fill-in the *Table of Stops and Fricatives*:

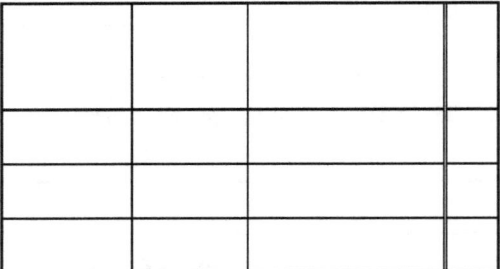

3

Articles, Prepositions, and Third Declension Nouns

3.1 Articles

1. Greek, like English, distinguishes between definite ("the") and indefinite ("a") articles. True or False
2. Greek articles exhibit case, number, and gender because they are declinable. True or False
3. List the three Greek articles (lexical form) and their gender.

   a. ___ _____ _____
   b. ___ _____ _____
   c. ___ _____ _____

4. The article of a word and the word itself must always be identical in _____, _____, and _____.
5. A word that is *anarthrous* has an article. True or False
6. A word that is *articular* has an article. True or False

7. Fill-in the *Table of Articles*:

	2nd	1st	2nd
	Masc	Fem	Neut
Sg Nom			
Sg Gen			
Sg Dat			
Sg Acc			
Pl Nom			
Pl Gen			
Pl Dat			
Pl Acc			

8. Articles can serve to
    a. Distinguish
    b. Substitute
    c. Function as a pronoun
    d. All of the above

3.2 Prepositions

1. Prepositions are words that
   _____.
2. Prepositions usually indicate a _____ or _____ relationship.
3. Indicate (circle/underline) all the prepositions in the following English sentences:
    a. The cat sat on the mat.
    b. The pastor likes to preach from the pulpit.

c. Bullets were flying everywhere, from the bunks and over the hills, behind the trees and under the bushes.
   d. When they went home, they studied Greek on their beds.
4. Indicate the preposition in the following sentence: καὶ ὁ θεὸς ἐν αὐτῷ μένει.
5. The word following a preposition is called the _____ of the preposition.
6. The word following a preposition is usually in the _____ or _____ case.
7. Prepositions are not inflected, so they generally don't change. True or False
8. "Elision" is when a preposition ends with a vowel and the following word begins with a vowel. Example: μετὰ αὐτοῦ = _____
9. Identify the original preposition that underwent elision in the following examples, and then translate the phrase:
   a. κατ' ἐξουσίαν (κατὰ): according to authority[14]
   b. μετ' ἀλλήλων (_____): _____[15]
   c. ὑπ' οὐρανὸν (___): _____[16]
   d. παρ' ἐλπίδα (_____): _____[17]
   e. δι' ἐπαγγελίας (___): _____[18]
10. Prepositions can have multiple meanings. True or False
11. The meaning of prepositions may depend on the case of the object of the preposition. True or False
12. Some prepositions can have several meanings. Complete the following:
    a. δια = _____ (gen); _____, _____ (acc)

---

[14] Mk 1:27.
[15] Lk 23:12; Jn 6:43; 1 Jn 1:7.
[16] Lk 17:24.
[17] Rom 4:18.
[18] Gal 3:18; 4:23.

b. μετά = _____, _____ (gen); _____, _____ (acc)

c. ὑπέρ = _____, _____ (gen); _____, _____ (acc)

d. ὑπο = _____, _____ (gen); _____, _____ (acc)

e. περί = _____, _____ (gen); _____ (acc)

f. παρά = _____ (the side of) (gen); _____, _____ (dat); _____, _____ (acc)

g. πρός = _____, _____ (acc); _____ (gen); _____, _____ (dat)

h. κατά = throughout, down (from/along); _____, _____ (gen); _____, _____, _____ (acc)

13. Some prepositions have only one meaning. Complete the following:

a. ἀπό = _____ (___)

b. ἐκ, ἐξ = _____ (___)

c. σύν = _____ (___)

3.3 Third Declension Nouns

1. Third Declension Nouns have stems ending in a _____.

2. Fill-in the completed *Table of Case Endings*:

	2ⁿᵈ	1ˢᵗ	2ⁿᵈ	3ʳᵈ	
	Masc	Fem	Neut	M/F	Neut
Sg Nom					
Sg Gen					
Sg Dat					
Sg Acc					
Pl Nom					
Pl Gen					
Pl Dat					
Pl Acc					

3. Complete the following:
   a. σαρκ + σι = _____
   b. σκολοπ + σ = _____
   c. ονοματ + σι = _____
4. It is easy to find the stem of a third declension noun without having memorized the genitive form. True or False
5. List the Five Rules of the Third Declension:
   1. _____
   2. _____
   3. _____
   4. _____
   5. _____

Vocabulary

ἀλλά
ἀπό [ἀπ', ἀφ']
διά
ἐκ, ἐξ
ἡμέρα, -ας, ἡ
θάλασσα, -ης, ἡ
θάνατος, -ου, ὁ
ἵνα
Ἰωάννης, -ου, ὁ
λέγω
μετά [μετ', μεθ']
οἰκία, -ας, ἡ
οἶκος, -ου, ὁ
ὄχλος, -ου, ὁ
παρά
πρός
ὑπό [ὑπ', ὑφ']
ἅγιος, -ία, -ιον
ἀνήρ, ἀνδρός, ὁ
εἰ
εἷς, μία, ἕν
ἤδη
ὄνομα, -ατος, τό
πατήρ, πατρός
περί
πίστις, -τεως, ἡ
σάρξ, σαρκός, ἡ
σύν
σῶμα, -ατος, τό

τέκνον, -ου, τό _____
ὑπέρ _____
ὕδωρ, ὕδατος, τό _____
φῶς, φωτός, τό _____
χάρις, -ιτος, ἡ _____
πᾶς, πᾶσα, πᾶν _____
τις, τι _____
τίς, τί _____
κατα _____

_____ 1) favor, grace; 2) favor, grace, beneficence, blessing; 3) expression of requital, thanks

_____ all, whole, each, every(one/thing/body), every kind/sort (of)

_____ pron. someone, anyone, one, a certain one, a somebody, certain (ones), some, something, anything, any, a certain

_____ 1) who?, what?, why?, what, which; 2) why?, how!

_____ but, on the other hand, yet, nevertheless, indeed, certainly

_____ prep. 1) w. gen. by, at the hands of, from; 2) w. acc. below, under, next to, at, about, subject to

_____ prep. 1) w. gen. for, in behalf of, in the interest of, in place of, instead of, in the name of, because of, for the sake, about, concerning, with regard to; 2) w. acc. above, beyond, over, more than, than, even more

_____ water

_____ 1) child; 2) descendants, posterity, son; 3) child

_____ 1) body, corpse; 2) body

_____ prep. w. dat. with, along with, including, as well as, besides/not only all this

_____ 1) flesh, human being, person; 2) old self

_____ death

_____ 1) sea; 2) lake

_____ prep. 1) w. acc. to, toward, for, next to, at, against, with a view to, in view of, with, before, relating to, pertaining to, in reference to, in keeping with, regarding, relative to, compared to, with x in mind, for the benefit of x, against; 2) w. gen. in the interest of; 3) w. dat. at, close by, near

_____ 1) faithfulness, fidelity, promise, guarantee, pledge; 2) faith, trust, confidence, conviction

_____ prep. about; a) w. gen. about, concerning, for; b) w. acc. with, in connection with, about, around, near

_____ 1) father, parents; 2) ancestor, forebear; 3-5) father

_____ prep. 1) w. gen. from (the side of); 2) w. dat. with, in association with, in the presence of, among, beside, next to, near; 3) w. acc. alongside, near, at, by, beside, in contrast to, in preference to, contrary to, beyond

_____ 1) house, 2) household, family

_____ 1) house, home, dwelling; 2) house, household, family

_____ 1) name; 2) person

_____ crowd

_____ prep. w. gen. and w. acc. 1) throughout, down (from/along), along, toward, to, as far as; 2) w. gen. (swear) by; 3) w. gen. against; 4-5) w. acc. in line with, in accordance with, in keeping with; 6) w. acc. for, as a result of; 7) w. acc. according to

_____ prep. 1) w. gen. with, amid, among, in the company of, along with; 2) w. acc: after, behind

_____ a) say; b) refer to, talk (about), mention; c) call, name, a.k.a., mean(s)

_____ John

_____ 1) in order that; 2-3) that

_____ 1) day; 2) day(s); time

_____ adv. now, already

_____	1) light; 2) torch, lamp, fire, sun, heavenly bodies
_____	prep. w. gen: a) from, out of; by, from *x* on; b) at; c) for
_____	1) if; 2) if, whether
_____	one; 1) one, one and the same, first; 2) someone
_____	prep. through; a) w. gen. through; b) w. acc. through, because of
_____	prep. w. gen. from
_____	man
_____	holy

Parsing

Inflected	Case	Number	Gender	Lexical Form	Gloss
1. πατέρα					
2. παραβολὴν					
3. ἀνδράσιν					
4. οἰκίᾳ					
5. ὄχλον					
6. ἡμέραι					
7. θάλασσαν					
8. φωτὸς					
9. φωνὴ					
10. σώματα					
11. χάριτος					
12. ὀνόματι					
13. πίστεως					
14. ὕδασιν					
15. τέκνα					
16. θανάτῳ					
17. ζωῆς					
18. καρδίαις					
19. προφῆται					

Translation

1. ...ἄνδρα πλήρης (full) πίστεως καὶ πνεύματος ἁγίου.[19]

2. Τίς ἐστιν ὁ ἄνθρωπος ...?[20] _____

3. ἵνα ὥσπερ (just as) ἐβασίλευσεν (reigned) ἡ ἁμαρτία ἐν τῷ θανάτῳ, οὕτως καὶ ἡ χάρις βασιλεύσῃ (to rule) διὰ δικαιοσύνης εἰς ζωὴν αἰώνιον διὰ Ἰησοῦ Χριστοῦ τοῦ κυρίου ἡμῶν.[21]

4. ...κτισθέντες (created) ἐν Χριστῷ Ἰησοῦ ἐπὶ ἔργοις ἀγαθοῖς (good) οἷς (which) προητοίμασεν (prepared) ὁ θεὸς ἵνα ἐν αὐτοῖς περιπατήσωμεν (we should walk).[22]

5. αὐτοὶ (they) ἐκ τοῦ κόσμου εἰσίν· διὰ τοῦτο ἐκ τοῦ κόσμου λαλοῦσιν (they speak) καὶ ὁ κόσμος αὐτῶν ἀκούει (listens).[23]

6. ἀδελφοί· μόνον (only) μὴ τὴν (use)[24] ἐλευθερίαν (freedom) εἰς ἀφορμὴν (opportunity) τῇ σαρκί, ἀλλὰ διὰ τῆς ἀγάπης δουλεύετε (serve) ἀλλήλοις.[25]

7. ...καὶ ὀφθήσεται (will be seen) ἐν ὑμῖν (among you) δόξα κυρίου.[26]

---

[19] Acts 6:5.
[20] Jn 5:12.
[21] Rom 5:21.
[22] Eph 2:10.
[23] 1 Jn 4:5.
[24] This verb has to be supplied; see also "turn" in NASB.
[25] Gal 5:13.
[26] Lev 9:6, LXX.

8. ὅτι ἐξ αὐτοῦ (him) καὶ δι' αὐτοῦ καὶ εἰς αὐτὸν τὰ πάντα· αὐτῷ ἡ δόξα εἰς τοὺς αἰῶνας (eternal)· ἀμήν.[27]

_____

9. ἀλλ' ἡμῖν (for us) εἷς θεὸς ὁ πατήρ, ἐξ οὗ (whom) τὰ πάντα καὶ ἡμεῖς (we) εἰς αὐτόν, καὶ εἷς κύριος Ἰησοῦς Χριστός, δι' οὗ (whom) τὰ πάντα καὶ ἡμεῖς δι' αὐτοῦ.[28]

_____

10. εἰ γὰρ κατὰ σάρκα ζῆτε (you live) μέλλετε ἀποθνῄσκειν (you will die), εἰ δὲ πνεύματι τὰς πράξεις (deeds) τοῦ σώματος θανατοῦτε (you put to death) ζήσεσθε (you will live).[29]

_____

11. ἦλθον (I have come) γὰρ διχάσαι (to set against) ἄνθρωπον κατὰ τοῦ πατρὸς αὐτοῦ καὶ θυγατέρα (daughter) κατὰ τῆς μητρὸς αὐτῆς…[30]

_____

12. Πάτερ ἡμῶν (our) ὁ ἐν τοῖς οὐρανοῖς, ἁγιασθήτω (make holy) τὸ ὄνομά σου.[31]

_____

13. Ὁ (whoever) φιλῶν (loves) πατέρα ἢ μητέρα ὑπὲρ ἐμὲ οὐκ ἔστιν μου ἄξιος (worthy).[32]

_____

---

[27] Rm 11:36. Remember from chapter 2 and the "predicate nominative," that the verb "to be" (is, am, are, exist) can be supplied.
[28] 1 Cor 8:6.
[29] Rm 8:13.
[30] Mt 10:35.
[31] Mt 6:9.
[32] Mt 10:37.

Review of Chapter 2

Write out the **Three Rules of Declensions**:

1. _____
2. _____
3. _____

Write out the **Four Rules of First and Second Declension Nouns**:

1. _____
2. _____
   _____
3. _____
4. _____

4

Adjectives and Adverbs

4.1-4.5 Introduction and Functions of Adjectives

1. An adjective is a word that modifies a noun, verb, or participle. True or False
2. Adjectives can be _____, _____, and even _____.
3. When modifying nouns, an adjective must match the _____, _____, and _____ of the noun it is modifying.
4. Match the following types of nouns with their description:
    a. "Justice is good." ___. Attributive Function
    b. "His head is huge." ___. Predicate Function
    c. "The meek will inherit the earth." ___. Substantival Function
5. The key to determining the function of an adjective is by _____.

    a. An adjective functions like an *attribute* if the article comes before the _____.
    b. An adjective functions like a *predicate* if the article comes before the _____, (and not before the adjective).
    c. An adjective functions like a noun if there is ___ _____ to modify.

6. Match the following texts with the type of adjective they are:
    a. "ὅτι ὁ θεὸς ἀληθής ἐστιν."[33]   __. First Predicate Position
    b. "πιστὸς δὲ ὁ θεὸς."[34]   __. Third Attrib. Position
    c. "τῆς δωρεᾶς τῆς ἐπουρανίου."[35]   __. Second Attrib. Position
    d. "στολὴν τὴν πρώτην"[36]   __. First Attrib. Position
    e. "ὁ ἀγαθὸς ἄνθρωπος"[37]   __. Second Predic. Position

4.6   Patterns of Adjectives

1. Match the four adjective patterns with the following vocabulary entries:
    a. κακός, -ή, όν   __. 2-2
    b. πονηρός, -ά, -όν[38]   __. 2-1-2
    c. τίς, τί   __. 3-1-3
    d. αἰώνιος, -ον   __. 3-3

4.7 Adjectival Degrees

1. "Largest" and "best" is an example of comparative degree. True or False.
2. Positive degree is a focus on _____.
3. Comparative degree usually compares ____ things.
4. Superlative degree usually involves _____ things.
5. Elative adjectives describe an _____ of the positive notion, usually translating with the word "very."

---

[33] Jn 3:33.
[34] 2 Cor 1:18.
[35] Heb 6:4.
[36] Lk 15:22.
[37] Lk 6:45.
[38] Recall the common third-declension roots ending in rho (ὕδωρ, μήτρη, etc.). And also ask: what is a more likely second-declension stem: κακο or πονηρο? These two clues should help you figure out which is a 3-1-3 and which is a 2-1-2.

4.8 Adverbs

1. Adverbs are words that modify or describe _____.
2. Most Greek adverbs end in –___.

Vocabulary

ἀγαθός, -ή, -όν _____
ἀγαπητός, -ή, -όν _____
αἰώνιος, -ον _____
ἀλλήλων _____
ἀπεκρίθη _____
δοῦλος, -ου, ὁ _____
ἐάν _____
ἐμός, ἐμή, ἐμόν _____
ἐντολή, -ῆς, ἡ _____
καθώς _____
κακός, -ή, -όν _____
μοῦ _____
νεκρός, -ά, -όν _____
παραβολή, -ῆς, ἡ _____
πιστός, -ή, -όν _____
πονηρός, -ά, -όν _____
πρῶτος, -η, -ον _____
τρίτος, -η, -ον _____
ἀδελφός, -οῦ, ὁ _____
ἄν _____
εἰ μή _____
ἐκκλησία, -ας, ἡ _____
ἔξω _____

ἐπί [ἐπ', ἐφ]	_____
ἡμεῖς	_____
θέλημα, -ματος, τό	_____
Ἰδέ; ἰδού	_____
καλός, -ή, -όν	_____
μήτηρ, μητρός, ἡ	_____
οὐδέ	_____
οὐδείς, οὐδεμία, οὐδέν	_____
ὑμεῖς	_____
ὧδε	_____

_____	"a multivalent marker that nuances verbs with an aspect of contingency or generalization"; would, ever, might
_____	1) long ages ago; 2) eternal; 3) permanent, lasting
_____	brother
_____	beloved
_____	good, useful
_____	each other, one another, mutually
_____	he/she/it answered (3rd pers. sg. aor. ἀποκρίνομαι)
_____	slave
_____	adv. outside; a) out(side), prep. w. gen. out (of/from); b) w. art. those outside, outsiders
_____	(if not); except, unless
_____	if
_____	1) assembly; 2) assembly, congregation
_____	1st pers. poss. pron. my, mine
_____	commandment, order, instruction

_____ prep. 1a) w. gen. on, over, at, before, in the presence of, on the basis of; 1b) w. dat. on, over, at, because of, on top of, in addition to, to, on the basis of, near, in regard to, about, along the lines of, for, against; 1c) w. acc. over, upon, on, against, up to, to, at, toward, in addition to, to, for; 2a) w. gen. in/at the time of, In the course of, at; 2b) w. dat. at the time of, at, on, over a period of, for; 3) w. dat. in

_____ we (nom. pl. ἐγώ)

_____ (you) see!; behold, look, see (impv. ὁράω/ εἶδον)

_____ 1) bad, something bad, a wrong; 2) harmful, bad

_____ fine, good

_____ a) as, just as; b) to the extent/degree that; c) inasmuch as, since

_____ mother

_____ my (gen. ἐγώ)

_____ dead one, corpse

_____ a) adj. no; b) n. no one, nobody, nothing, not a thing, in no way, not (be) worth consideration, amount to nothing

_____ a) no; b) neither, nor; c) not even, not; d-e) not even

_____ a) illustration, parable; b) symbol

_____ 1) reliable, faithful, truthworthy; 2) believing (with commitment), n. believer

_____ 1) bad, envious; 2) bad, poor; 3) bad, virulent

_____ 1) first, earlier, earliest, outer (part); 2) first, most prominent/important, first (of all)

_____ will, desire

_____ 1) third; 2) third part

_____ you (all) (nom. pl. σύ)

_____ adv. a) here, to this place, hither; b) here, in this place, in this connection

Parsing

Inflected	Case	Number	Gender	Lexical Form	Gloss
1. πάντες					
2. χάριτος					
3. ἀγαπητῷ					
4. δοῦλον					
5. ἐμά					
6. ἐντολῶν					
7. καλὸν					
8. κακαί					
9. πρώτου					
10. πιστός					
11. πονηρὰ					
12. νεκρῶν					
13. τρίτη					
14. ἐκκλησίας					
15. θέλημα					
16. μητέρες					
17. ἀλλήλους					
18. οὐδεμία					
19. ὄχλους					
20. παρά					

Translation

1. υἱὸν ἀγαπητόν.[39] _____
2. ὁ πιστὸς δοῦλος.[40] _____
3. μητέρες ἡμῶν ὡς αἱ χῆραι (widows).[41] _____
4. καὶ ἐφοβήθησαν (they were filled) φόβον μέγαν, καὶ ἔλεγον (said) πρὸς ἀλλήλους…[42]

   _____

5. καὶ εἶπεν (said) κύριος ὁ θεὸς τῇ γυναικί (woman/wife).[43]

   _____

6. Οἱ ἄνδρες, ἀγαπᾶτε (love) τὰς γυναῖκας.[44] _____
7. καὶ ἐγένετο (was) ἑσπέρα (evening) καὶ ἐγένετο πρωί, ἡμέρα τρίτη.[45]

   _____

8. καὶ ἐξεπορεύετο (going out) πρὸς αὐτὸν πᾶσα ἡ Ἰουδαία χώρα καὶ οἱ Ἱεροσολυμῖται πάντες, καὶ ἐβαπτίζοντο (were being baptized) ὑπ' αὐτοῦ ἐν τῷ Ἰορδάνῃ ποταμῷ (river) ἐξομολογούμενοι (confessing) τὰς ἁμαρτίας αὐτῶν.[46]

   _____

   _____

9. Ἡ μὲν οὖν ἐκκλησία καθ' ὅλης (all) τῆς Ἰουδαίας καὶ Γαλιλαίας καὶ Σαμαρείας εἶχεν (had) εἰρήνην, οἰκοδομουμένη (being built up) καὶ πορευομένη (walking) τῷ φόβῳ τοῦ κυρίου, καὶ τῇ παρακλήσει (encouragement) τοῦ ἁγίου πνεύματος ἐπληθύνετο (had grown).[47]

---

[39] Mk 12:6.
[40] Mt 24:45.
[41] Lam 5:3b, LXX.
[42] Mk 4:41.
[43] Gen 3:13, LXX.
[44] Col 3:19.
[45] Gen 1:13, LXX.
[46] Mk 1:5.
[47] Acts 9:31.

10. Ἰδοὺ δέδωκα (I have set) πρὸ προσώπου σου σήμερον τὴν ζωὴν καὶ τὸν θάνατον, τὸ ἀγαθὸν καὶ τὸ κακόν.[48]

11. Ἡ βασιλεία ἡ ἐμὴ οὐκ ἔστιν ἐκ τοῦ κόσμου τούτου.[49]

12. ὁ δὲ δοῦλος οὐ μένει (remains) ἐν τῇ οἰκίᾳ εἰς τὸν αἰῶνα· ὁ υἱὸς μένει εἰς τὸν αἰῶνα.[50]

13. Τιμοθέῳ ἀγαπητῷ τέκνῳ· χάρις, ἔλεος (mercy), εἰρήνη ἀπὸ θεοῦ πατρὸς καὶ Χριστοῦ Ἰησοῦ τοῦ κυρίου ἡμῶν (our).[51]

14. ὅτι ἐκ τοῦ πληρώματος (fullness) αὐτοῦ ἡμεῖς (we) πάντες ἐλάβομεν (have received), καὶ χάριν ἀντὶ (upon) χάριτος.[52]

15. νῦν γὰρ ἔγνων (I know) ὅτι φοβῇ (you fear) τὸν θεόν.[53]

16. ...γινώσκομεν (you know) ὅτι ἐσχάτη ὥρα ἐστίν.[54]

17. οἱ ὀφθαλμοί (eye) μου ἐπὶ τοὺς πιστούς.[55]

---

[48] Dt 30:15, LXX.
[49] Jn 18:36.
[50] Jn 8:35.
[51] 2 Tm 1:2.
[52] Jn 1:16.
[53] Gen 22:12.
[54] 1 Jn 2:18.
[55] Ps 101:6, LXX.

18. ὁ ἀγαθὸς ἄνθρωπος ἐκ τοῦ ἀγαθοῦ θησαυροῦ (treasure) ἐκβάλλει (brings forth) ἀγαθά, καὶ ὁ πονηρὸς ἄνθρωπος ἐκ τοῦ πονηροῦ θησαυροῦ ἐκβάλλει πονηρά.[56]

19. ἐὰν δὲ μὴ πιστεύσωσίν (believe) σοι μηδὲ εἰσακούσωσιν (give ear to) τῆς φωνῆς τοῦ σημείου τοῦ πρώτου, πιστεύσουσίν σοι τῆς φωνῆς τοῦ σημείου τοῦ ἐσχάτου.[57]

20. ὁ δὲ θεὸς ἤγειρεν (raised) αὐτὸν ἐκ νεκρῶν·[58]

21. οὐχ οὕτως ὁ θεράπων (attendant) μου Μωυσῆς· ἐν ὅλῳ (whole) τῷ οἴκῳ μου πιστός ἐστιν·[59]

22. ...καὶ ἡ φωνὴ τῶν λόγων αὐτοῦ ὡς φωνὴ ὄχλου.[60]

---

[56] Mt 12:35.
[57] Ex 4:8, LXX.
[58] Acts 13:30. Note that the noun "the dead" can function as both singular and plural in English, and that "the dead" in a NT context is more of a realm that exhibits plurality than is actually indicating an immediate presence of dead ones.
[59] Num 12:7, LXX.
[60] Dan 10:6, LXX.

5

Personal Pronouns

5.1 Introduction

1. Pronouns can _____ for nouns, as well as _____ and _____.
2. The most common type of pronoun in the New Testament are _____ pronouns.

5.2 The Grammar of Pronouns

1. The case of a pronoun is determined by _____.
2. The gender and number of a pronoun is determined by its _____.
3. Identify the antecedent (circle/underline/highlight) of the underlined pronouns in the following sentences:
    a. "Jack says <u>he's</u> addicted to Diet Coke; I think <u>he's</u> telling the truth."
    b. "Don't mind <u>her</u>. My sister is always a little picky about food."

4. Pronouns are in _____, _____, and _____ person:
   a. The person speaking (_____)
   b. The person beign spoken about (_____)
   c. The person being spoken to (_____)
5. Identify the person in the underlined words below:
   a. "Henry went home to play with <u>his</u> kids." _____
   b. "<u>You</u> were not telling the truth; <u>you</u> were all lying." _____
   c. "<u>They</u> didn't tell you I was on vacation?" _____
   d. "They didn't tell you <u>I</u> was on vacation?" _____
   e. "They didn't tell <u>you</u> I was on vacation?" _____
   f. "<u>We</u> realize you didn't understand the rules." _____
   g. "We realize <u>you</u> didn't understand the rules." _____

5.3 First and Second Person Pronouns

1. Second person pronouns in Greek do not exhibit gender. True or False.
2. Fill out the following table with the proper English pronouns:

1ˢᵗ Person		2ⁿᵈ Person	
ἐγώ		σύ	
μου (ἐμοῦ)		σου (σοῦ)	
μοι (ἐμοί)		σοι (σοί)	
με (ἐμέ)		σε (σέ)	
ἡμεῖς		ὑμεῖς	
ἡμῶν		ὑμῶν	
ἡμῖν		ὑμῖν	
ἡμᾶς		ὑμᾶς	

3. The _____ forms of pronouns usually come after the word they modify.
4. Do translations differ in their rendering of pronouns for 1 Peter 3:18? If so, why do you think? What translation would you prefer and why?

_____
_____
_____
_____
_____

5.4 Third Person Pronoun

1. The third person pronoun in Greek is _____, which follows the pattern _____.
2. αὐτός has three major functions: **(1)** _____ _____, **(2)** _____ _____, **(3)** _____ _____.
3. Match the following sentences with their use of αὐτός:
    a. "Geitner <u>himself</u> even admits bankruptcy."   ___. Personal Pronoun
    b. "<u>His</u> garden is huge!"   ___. Adjectival Intens.
    c. "At the <u>same</u> time they fell in the water."   ___. Identical Adjective

4. Fill out the *Table of Personal Pronouns*:

1st	2nd	3rd M	3rd F	3rd N

Vocabulary

αἰών, -ῶνος, ὁ
διδάσκαλος, -ου, ὁ
εὐθύς
ἕως
μαθητής, -ου, ὁ
μέν
μηδείς, μηδεμία, μηδέν
μόνος, -η, -ον
ὅπως
ὅσος, -η, -ον
οὖν
ὀφθαλμός, -οῦ, ὁ
πάλιν
πούς, ποδός, ὁ
γυνή, γυναικος, ἡ
δικαιοσύνη, -ης, ἡ
δώδεκα
ἑαυτοῦ, -ῆς, -οῦ
ἐκεῖνος, -η, -ο
ἐλπίς, ίδος, ἡ
ἤ
κἀγώ
μακάριος, -ια, -ιον
μέγας, μεγάλη, μέγα and μείζων, -ον
πόλις, -εως, ἡ
πολύς, πολλή, πολύ or πλείων, πλεῖον, πλέον
πῶς

σημεῖον, -ου, τό _____

_____ 1) in the past, ages ago, eternity; 2) age; 3) world; 4) Aeon
_____ teacher, instructor
_____ uprightness, righteousness, justice
_____ twelve
_____ 1) till, until, as long as, while; 2) as far as, to, until, (up) to, until
_____ reflex. pron. 1) self/selves; 2) each other, one another; 3) poss. pron. his, her, their
_____ dem. pron. that (person/thing) (pl. those)
_____ 1) hope, expectation; 2-3) hope
_____ adv. immediately, at once
_____ 1) woman; 2) wife
_____ 1) or, either…or; 2) than, rather; before
_____ and I; (and) I too/also/in turn, On my part, I on the other hand, as for me
_____ blessed, privileged, fortunate, happy
_____ a) pupil; b) adherent, disciple
_____ great, greater, very exceptional, outstanding
_____ a) on the one hand/indeed/now…but, one…another, some…others, at times…at other times; b) now, so then, rather
_____ 1) adj. no, any; 2) n. nobody, nothing, anything, not…at all, in no way, without…at all
_____ a) adj. alone, only; b) adv. merely, just, only
_____ how, that, in order that
_____ 1) as much as, as long as; 2) as many (much) as, all who, whatever/everything that; 3) to the degree/extent that
_____ eye, sight
_____ ppos. a) so, then, hence; b) then, now, so, in turn

Chapter Five: Personal Pronouns

_____ adv. a) again, once more, on the other hand, in turn, what's more, moreoever; b) back

_____ a) adj. pl. many; b) adj. much, great, long, greater, still more, longer, many, most, large, big, immense, vast; c) n. many things, much, adv. greatly, many, the many, most

_____ foot

_____ a) city, town; b) inhabitants

_____ adv. 1) how?, in what manner/way?, how is it then?, how can it be that?, by what right?, in what sense?; 2) how!

_____ sign

Parsing

Inflected	Case	Number	Gender	Lexical Form	Gloss
1. διδασκάλων					
2. μηδενὶ					
3. μαθηταὶ					
4. ὅσοι					
5. μόνον					
6. αἰῶσιν					
7. ὀφθαλμοῖς					
8. πόδα					
9. δικαιοσύνην					
10. πολὺ					
11. ἑαυτοῖς					
12. ἐκείνῳ					
13. ἐλπίδα					
14. Μακαρία					
15. μεγάλους					
16. σημεῖον					
17. πολλά					
18. αὐτῆς					
19. γυναῖκας					
20. αὐτῶν					

Translation

1. φόβητρά (terrors) τε καὶ ἀπ' οὐρανοῦ σημεῖα μεγάλα ἔσται (will be).[61]

2. καὶ ὑπὲρ πάντων ἀπέθανεν (died) ἵνα οἱ ζῶντες (live) μηκέτι (no longer) ἑαυτοῖς ζῶσιν (live) ἀλλὰ τῷ ὑπὲρ αὐτῶν ἀποθανόντι (died) καὶ ἐγερθέντι (was raised).[62]

3. καὶ εἶπεν Λεια Μακαρία ἐγώ, ὅτι μακαρίζουσίν (pronounce) με αἱ γυναῖκες· καὶ ἐκάλεσεν (called) τὸ ὄνομα αὐτοῦ Ασηρ.[63]

4. καὶ ἐποίησεν (made) ὁ θεὸς τοὺς δύο φωστῆρας (luminaries) τοὺς μεγάλους.[64]

5. …κατὰ τὴν ἀποκαραδοκίαν (eager expectation) καὶ ἐλπίδα μου ὅτι ἐν οὐδενὶ αἰσχυνθήσομαι (I will be ashamed), ἀλλ' ἐν πάσῃ παρρησίᾳ (courage) ὡς πάντοτε (always) καὶ νῦν μεγαλυνθήσεται (will be honored) Χριστὸς ἐν τῷ σώματί μου, εἴτε διὰ ζωῆς εἴτε διὰ θανάτου.[65]

6. Μακάριοι οἱ πτωχοὶ (poor) τῷ πνεύματι, ὅτι αὐτῶν ἐστιν ἡ βασιλεία τῶν οὐρανῶν.[66]

---

[61] Lk 21:11.
[62] 2 Cor 5:15.
[63] Gen 30:13, LXX.
[64] Gen 1:16, LXX.
[65] Php 1:20.
[66] Mt 5:3.

7. μακάριος ὁ δοῦλος ἐκεῖνος ὃν (whom) ἐλθὼν (comes) ὁ κύριος αὐτοῦ εὑρήσει (will find) οὕτως ποιοῦντα (doing)·[67]

8. θησαυρίζετε (lay up) δὲ ὑμῖν θησαυροὺς (treasures) ἐν οὐρανῷ, ὅπου οὔτε σὴς (moth) οὔτε βρῶσις (rust) ἀφανίζει (destroy), καὶ ὅπου κλέπται (thieves) οὐ διορύσσουσιν (break in) οὐδὲ κλέπτουσιν (steal)·[68]

9. ὅπου γάρ ἐστιν ὁ θησαυρός σου, ἐκεῖ ἔσται (will be) καὶ ἡ καρδία σου.[69]

10. Ὁ λύχνος (lamp) τοῦ σώματός ἐστιν ὁ ὀφθαλμός. ἐὰν οὖν ᾖ ὁ ὀφθαλμός σου ἁπλοῦς (sincere), ὅλον τὸ σῶμά σου φωτεινὸν (shining) ἔσται· ἐὰν δὲ ὁ ὀφθαλμός σου πονηρὸς ᾖ, ὅλον τὸ σῶμά σου σκοτεινὸν (dark) ἔσται. εἰ οὖν τὸ φῶς τὸ ἐν σοὶ σκότος (darkness) ἐστίν, τὸ σκότος πόσον.[70]

11. ὁ μὲν υἱὸς τοῦ ἀνθρώπου ὑπάγει (goes) καθὼς γέγραπται (it is written) περὶ αὐτοῦ, οὐαὶ (woe) δὲ τῷ ἀνθρώπῳ ἐκείνῳ δι' οὗ ὁ υἱὸς τοῦ ἀνθρώπου παραδίδοται (is betrayed)· καλὸν ἦν αὐτῷ εἰ οὐκ ἐγεννήθη (was born) ὁ ἄνθρωπος ἐκεῖνος.[71]

12. ὅτι ἀνήρ ἐστιν κεφαλὴ (head/hair) τῆς γυναικὸς ὡς καὶ ὁ Χριστὸς κεφαλὴ τῆς ἐκκλησίας, αὐτὸς σωτὴρ (savior) τοῦ σώματος.[72]

---

[67] Mt 24:46.
[68] Mt 6:19.
[69] Mt 6:21.
[70] Mt 6:22-23. ᾖ here is actually a subjunctive (expressing a probability/possibility) form of εἰμι.
[71] Mt 26:24.
[72] Eph 5:23.

13. μᾶλλον (more) δὲ προσετίθεντο (were added) πιστεύοντες τῷ κυρίῳ πλήθη (multitudes) ἀνδρῶν τε καὶ γυναικῶν.[73]

14. Κατακολουθήσασαι (were following after) δὲ αἱ γυναῖκες, αἵτινες (who) ἦσαν (were) συνεληλυθυῖαι (traveling) ἐκ τῆς Γαλιλαίας αὐτῷ, ἐθεάσαντο (saw) τὸ μνημεῖον (tomb) καὶ ὡς ἐτέθη (placed) τὸ σῶμα αὐτοῦ,[74]

15. ἀκούοντα (heard) δὲ τὰ ἔθνη ἔχαιρον (rejoicing) καὶ ἐδόξαζον (glorifying) τὸν λόγον τοῦ κυρίου, καὶ ἐπίστευσαν (believed) ὅσοι ἦσαν (they were) τεταγμένοι (were designated) εἰς ζωὴν αἰώνιον·[75]

16. Καὶ εἶπεν (said) κύριος ὁ θεός Οὐ καλὸν εἶναι (exists) τὸν ἄνθρωπον μόνον.[76]

17. ᾔδει (see) γὰρ ὁ θεὸς ὅτι ἐν ᾗ ἂν ἡμέρᾳ φάγητε (you eat) ἀπ' αὐτοῦ, διανοιχθήσονται (will be opened) ὑμῶν οἱ ὀφθαλμοί, καὶ ἔσεσθε (you will be) ὡς θεοὶ γινώσκοντες (knowing) καλὸν καὶ πονηρόν. καὶ εἶδεν (saw) ἡ γυνὴ ὅτι καλὸν τὸ ξύλον (tree) εἰς βρῶσιν (eating) καὶ ὅτι ἀρεστὸν (pleasing) τοῖς ὀφθαλμοῖς ἰδεῖν (saw)…[77]

---

[73] Acts 5:14.
[74] Lk 23:55.
[75] Acts 13:48.
[76] Gen 2:18, LXX.
[77] Gen 3:5-6a, LXX.

18. ὁ γὰρ κύριος ἔσται (will be) ἐπὶ πασῶν ὁδῶν σου καὶ ἐρείσει (support) σὸν (your) πόδα, ἵνα μὴ σαλευθῇς (be unsettled).[78]

19. ...οἳ (who) διὰ πίστεως κατηγωνίσαντο (conquered) βασιλείας, εἰργάσαντο (enforced) δικαιοσύνην, ἐπέτυχον (obtained) ἐπαγγελιῶν[79]

20. γυναῖκας ὡσαύτως σεμνάς (dignified), μὴ διαβόλους (slanderers), νηφαλίους (sober-minded), πιστὰς ἐν πᾶσιν.[80]

21. καὶ κύριος καθαριεῖ (will forgive) αὐτήν, ὅτι ἀνένευσεν (opposed) ὁ πατὴρ αὐτῆς.[81]

---

[78] Prv 3:26, LXX.
[79] Heb 11:33a.
[80] 1 Tim 3:11.
[81] Num 30:5.

6

Demonstrative and Relative Pronouns

6.1 Demonstrative Pronouns

1. Demonstrative pronouns function as both _____ and _____ in order to _____ something.
2. What is the difference between ouJ:toV, au{th, tou:to and ejkei:noV, ejkei:nh, ejkei:no, and how should they be translated?
   _____
   _____

   When functioning as *pronouns*, the case is determined by its _____ and its gender and number are determined by its _____.

3. When functioning as *adjectives*, the case, number, and gender are determined by _____.
4. Unlike normal adjectives, if there is an article before the noun, the demonstrative pronoun functions _____.
5. Demonstrative pronouns are *always* in the predicate position. True or False

6. Complete the *Table of Proximal Demonstrative Pronouns*:

M (2)	F (1)	N (2)
οὗτος	αὕτη	τοῦτο

7. Complete the *Table of Distal Demonstrative Pronouns*:

M (2)	F (1)	N (2)
ἐκεῖνος	ἐκείνη	ἐκεῖνο

6.2 Relative Pronouns

1. Relative pronouns relate to _____.
2. Like αὐτός, the number and gender of a relative pronoun (usually) matches the _____.
3. The case of the relative pronoun is determined its function in the _____.
4. The two relative pronouns are __, __, __ ("who," "whom," "that," "which," "whose") and _____, _____, _____ ("who," "which").
5. The definite relative pronoun in Greek is __ while the indefinite pronoun is _____.
6. If being used generically, ὅστις focuses _____.
7. If being used qualitatively, ὅστις focuses _____.
8. Complete the table below:

M	F	N	gloss
ὅς	ἥ	ὅ	

9. The key to identifying the relative pronoun is the
   _____.

10. Relative clauses stand alone; they are independent of the main subject and verb of the sentence. True or False

Vocabulary

ἀλήθεια, -ας, ἡ   _____
εἰρήνη, -ης, ἡ   _____
ἐνώπιον   _____
ἐπαγγελία, -ας, ἡ   _____
ἑπτά   _____
θρόνος, -ου, ὁ   _____
Ιερουσαλήμ, ἡ or
Ιερουσαλήμα, τά/ἡ   _____
κατά   _____
κεφαλή, -ῆς, ἡ   _____
ὁδός, -οῦ, ἡ   _____
ὅς, ἥ, ὅ   _____
ὅτε   _____
οὕτω/οὕτως   _____
πλοῖον, -ου, τό   _____
ῥῆμα, -ματος, τό   _____
χείρ, χειρός, ἡ   _____
ψυχή, -ῆς, ἡ   _____

_____ truth
_____ 1-2) hand
_____ 1-2) peace

Chapter Six: Demonstrative and Relative Pronouns

_____	prep. w. gen. a) ahead; b) in presence (of); c) in front (of); d) before, under, scrutiny, in sight (of); e) before promise
_____	seven
_____	Jerusalem
_____	prep. w. gen. and w. acc. 1) throughout, down (from/along), along, toward, to, as far as; 2) w. gen. (swear) by; 3) w. gen. against; 4-5) w. acc. in line with, in accordance with, in keeping with; 6) w. acc. for, as a result of; 7) w. acc. according to
_____	head
_____	who, which/what, that
_____	when, as long as, while
_____	1) way, road, highway, path; 2) way, journey, trip, the Way
_____	in this way/manner/fashion
_____	ship, boat
_____	throne, the enthroned
_____	1) statement, pronouncement, declaration; 2) a matter, thing, event
_____	1) life; 2) person, creature; 3) life, (inner) self, soul

Parsing

Inflected	Case	Number	Gender	Lexical Form	Gloss
1. εἰρήνης					
2. ἀληθείᾳ					
3. ἐπαγγελίαι					
4. ἐκείνων					
5. τοῦτο					
6. ὁδοῖς					
7. Ἱεροσόλυμα					
8. αἵ					
9. κεφαλάς					
10. πλοῖα					
11. ταύτης					
12. οὗ					
13. χεῖράς					
14. ἐκείνην					
15. τούτῳ					
16. ὁδῷ					
17. ἐκείνοις					
18. οὕς					
19. ῥήματα					
20. ψυχή					

Translation

1. αὕτη ἡ πόλις ἡ μεγάλη.[82] _____
2. Λέων (lion) ἐν ταῖς ὁδοῖς.[83] _____.
3. ἰδοὺ καὶ τὰ πλοῖα.[84] _____.
4. ἔσται (it will be) δὲ πᾶσα ψυχὴ ἥτις ἐὰν μὴ ἀκούσῃ (listen) τοῦ προφήτου ἐκείνου ἐξολεθρευθήσεται (will be destroyed) ἐκ τοῦ λαοῦ.[85]

    _____

5. Ἐπειδὴ (after) ἐπλήρωσεν (he finished) πάντα τὰ ῥήματα αὐτοῦ εἰς τὰς ἀκοὰς (the hearing) τοῦ λαοῦ, εἰσῆλθεν (he entered) εἰς Καφαρναούμ.[86]

    _____

6. Φέρε (place) τὸν δάκτυλόν (finger) σου ὧδε καὶ ἴδε τὰς χεῖράς μου, καὶ φέρε (place) τὴν χεῖρά σου καὶ βάλε (put) εἰς τὴν πλευράν (side) μου, καὶ μὴ γίνου (be) ἄπιστος (unbelieving) ἀλλὰ πιστός.[87]

    _____

7. σὺ δὲ ἀπελεύσῃ (depart) πρὸς τοὺς πατέρας σου μετ' εἰρήνης, ταφεὶς [pay last dues to corpse] ἐν γήρει [old age] καλῷ.[88]

    _____

8. ἃ καὶ λαλοῦμεν οὐκ ἐν διδακτοῖς ἀνθρωπίνης σοφίας λόγοις ἀλλ' ἐν διδακτοῖς πνεύματος, πνευματικοῖς πνευματικὰ συγκρίνοντες (understanding).[89]

    _____

---

[82] Gen 10:12, LXX. Compare the KJV, NET, and NRSV renderings.
[83] Prov 26:13, LXX.
[84] Js 3:4.
[85] Acts 3:23.
[86] Lk 7:1.
[87] Jn 20:27.
[88] Gen 15:15, LXX.
[89] 1 Cor 2:13.

9. λέγει αὐτῷ ὁ Ἰησοῦς, Ἐγώ εἰμι ἡ ὁδὸς καὶ ἡ ἀλήθεια καὶ ἡ ζωή· οὐδεὶς ἔρχεται (comes) πρὸς τὸν πατέρα εἰ μὴ δι' ἐμοῦ.[90]

10. ὅταν δὲ ἔλθῃ (comes) ἐκεῖνος, τὸ πνεῦμα τῆς ἀληθείας, ὁδηγήσει (he will guide) ὑμᾶς ἐν τῇ ἀληθείᾳ πάσῃ· οὐ γὰρ λαλήσει (he will speak) ἀφ' ἑαυτοῦ, ἀλλ' ὅσα ἀκούσει (he hears) λαλήσει, καὶ τὰ ἐρχόμενα ἀναγγελεῖ (will declare) ὑμῖν.[91]

11. ...ἀλλὰ ἔσονται πεποιθότες (will lean) ἐπὶ τὸν θεὸν τὸν ἅγιον τοῦ Ἰσραηλ τῇ ἀληθείᾳ,[92]

12. τῷ δὲ Ἀβραὰμ ἐρρέθησαν (said) αἱ ἐπαγγελίαι καὶ τῷ σπέρματι αὐτοῦ. οὐ λέγει, Καὶ τοῖς σπέρμασιν, ὡς ἐπὶ πολλῶν, ἀλλ' ὡς ἐφ' ἑνός, Καὶ τῷ σπέρματί σου, ὅς ἐστιν Χριστός.[93]

13. ὅτι ἐκεῖ ἐκάθισαν (were set) θρόνοι εἰς κρίσιν, θρόνοι ἐπὶ οἶκον Δαυιδ.[94]

14. αἱ ἑπτὰ βόες (cows) αἱ καλαὶ ἑπτὰ ἔτη (year) ἐστίν, καὶ οἱ ἑπτὰ στάχυες (ears) οἱ καλοὶ ἑπτὰ ἔτη ἐστίν· τὸ ἐνύπνιον (a thing seen in sleep) Φαραω ἕν ἐστιν.[95]

---

[90] Jn 14:6.
[91] Jn 16:13.
[92] Is 10:20, LXX.
[93] Gal 3:16.
[94] Ps 122:5, LXX.
[95] Gen 41:26, LXX.

15. ...λέγων (saying), Οὐ παραγγελίᾳ (commandment) παρηγγείλαμεν (charged) ὑμῖν μὴ διδάσκειν (teach) ἐπὶ τῷ ὀνόματι τούτῳ; καὶ ἰδοὺ πεπληρώκατε (filled) τὴν Ἰερουσαλὴμ τῆς διδαχῆς ὑμῶν, καὶ βούλεσθε (you intend) ἐπαγαγεῖν (to bring upon) ἐφ' ἡμᾶς τὸ αἷμα τοῦ ἀνθρώπου τούτου.[96]

16. αὐτός σου τηρήσει (will watch) κεφαλήν, καὶ σὺ τηρήσεις (will watch) αὐτοῦ πτέρναν (heel).[97]

17. Καὶ οὗτοι ἀρχηγοὶ οἴκων πατριῶν αὐτῶν.[98]

18. ...καὶ διηγήσατο (declared) αὐτοῖς πῶς ἐν τῇ ὁδῷ εἶδεν (had seen) τὸν κύριον καὶ ὅτι ἐλάλησεν (who had spoke) αὐτῷ, καὶ πῶς ἐν Δαμασκῷ ἐπαρρησιάσατο (he had preached) ἐν τῷ ὀνόματι τοῦ Ἰησοῦ.[99]

---

[96] Acts 5:28.
[97] Gen 3:15b, LXX.
[98] Ex 6:14a, LXX.
[99] Acts 9:27.

7

Introduction to Verbs and Present Active Indicative

7.1 Introduction to Verbs

1. Verbs have to agree with what they are modifying. True or False
2. Greek has three persons, first person (I), second person (you), and third person (he, she, it). True or False
3. Like English, Greek has three "persons" when it comes to verbs:
    a. The person speaking (_____)
    b. The person being spoken about (_____)
    c. The person being spoken to (_____)
4. Greek verbs are either singular (one) or plural (many). True or False
5. Match the following voices of Greek verbs:
    a. Active   ___. subject performs, produces, or experiences the action
    b. Middle   ___. Subject receives the action
    c. Passive   ___. Subject both performs…and receives the action

7.2 Table of Verb Endings

1. Fill-in the entire *Table of Verb Endings*:

		Primary Endings	*Secondary Endings*
Active Voice	Singular		
	Plural		
Midd/Pass Voice	Singular		
	Plural		

2. What is the major difference between the primary and secondary endings?
_____
_____

7.3 Additional Properties of Greek Verbs

1. Match the following properties of verbs:
   a. Time
   b. Tense
   c. Tense-Stem aspect
   d. Aspect

   ___. What type of action took place
   ___. When the action of the verb takes place
   ___. The general category of verbs, having time and
   ___. The grammatical *form* the verb takes

e. Mood   __. The speaker's attitude about relation of verb to reality

2. Match the following Greek moods:
   a. Subjunctive   __. Asserts something
   b. Indicative   __. Makes a command
   c. Imperative   __. Represents the verbal action as uncertain but probable

3. Match the following aspects of Greek verbs:
   a. Continuous   __. A simple event viewed as a whole
   b. Simple   __. Indicates incompleteness, progress, or process
   c. Completive   __. Views verb as brought to completion

4. Match the following components of a Greek verb:
   a. (Tense) Stem   __. suffixes at the end of a verb showing #, person, voice
   b. Connecting Vowel & Tense Formative   __. letters after the stem to make it easy to pronounce
   c. Personal endings.   __. The root of a verb in a given tense.

7.5 The Basic Form of Greek Verbs

1. What are the three elements that make up a typical Greek verb?

   _____ + _____ + _____

7.6 Present Active Indicative

1. The Present Active Indicative is an action that
   _____ _____
   It usually has the _____ aspect, though it can at times express a
   _____ aspect.

2. *Table of Verb Tenses*

Tense	Aug/Red	Tense stem	TF + CV	Endings	First singular
Pres mid/pas		pres	o/ε	prim mid/pas	λύομαι

3. *Table of Verb Endings*

		Primary Endings		Secondary Endings	
Active Voice	Singular			ἔλυον	ν/α
				ἔλυες	ς
				ἔλυε(ν)	(ν)
	Plural			ἐλύομεν	μεν
				ἐλύετε	τε
				ἔλυον	ν
Midd/Pass Voice	Singular	λύομαι	μαι	ἐλυόμην	μην
		λύῃ	σαι	ἐλύου	σο
		λύεται	ται	ἐλύετο	το
	Plural	λυόμεθα	μεθα	ἐλυόμεθα	μεθα
		λύεσθε	σθε	ἐλύεσθε	σθε
		λύονται	νται	ἐλύοντο	ντο

4. Paradigm of Present Active Indicative

	Form	Gloss	CV	Ending
1ˢᵗ Sg	λύω			
2ⁿᵈ Sg	λύεις			
3ʳᵈ Sg	λύει			
1ˢᵗ Pl	λύομεν			
2ⁿᵈ Pl	λύετε			
3ʳᵈ Pl	λύουσι(ν) [100]			

5. What determines whether the connecting vowel is an epsilon or an omega?
_____
_____

Vocabulary

ἀγαπάω   _____
ἀκούω   _____
βλέπω   _____
χαρά, -ᾶς, ἡ   _____
δαιμόνιον, -ου, τό _____
ἔχω   _____
καλέω   _____
λαλέω   _____
λύω   _____
νόμος, -ου, ὁ   _____
ὅταν   _____

---

[100] Note the contraction and lengthening of the omicron: ο + ο = ου.

Chapter Seven: Intro to Verbs and Present Active Indicative

ὅπου _____
οἶδα _____
πιστεύω _____
πληρόω _____
ποιέω _____
πρόσωπον, -ου, τό _____
τηρέω _____
τότε _____
τυφλός, -ή, όν _____
ζητέω _____

_____ 1) hear; 2) understand; 3) hear, hear about, pass. be said/rumored; 4) hear
_____ 1) be able to see; 2) see, look at, observe, watch, look on; 3) see, perceive, beware, be on guard (against), look out (for), heed; 4) look/face toward
_____ 1) have; 2) have (on), wear; 3) have wherewithal, be able; 4) consider, hold (to be), view; 5) have/be, be located, be near, be next, have to do with, relate to
_____ 1) loose, release, allow; 2) abolish; 3) break; 4) demolish, destroy
_____ 1) custom, norm, principle; 2) law
_____ adv. 1) where, wherever; 2) whereas
_____ 1) believe, give credence (to, about), have faith, be confident, put trust in, pl. n. believers; 2) entrust
_____ face, countenance, appearance
_____ temp. adv. a) then; b) at that time, then, thereupon
_____ 1-2) blind
_____ 1-2) joy
_____ I love, cherish
_____ 1) diety, divine being; 2) hostile/evil spirit, demon

	1) seek, look for; 2) deliberate, discuss; 3) desire, seek; 4) expect, demand
_____	1) seek, look for; 2) deliberate, discuss; 3) desire, seek; 4) expect, demand
_____	1) say, call, fall (for), summon; 2) call, invite; 3) call
_____	1) to sound, 2) speak (about), talk (about), tell, say, utter
_____	1) know; 2) perceive, understand
_____	a) whenever; b) when
_____	1) fill; 2) complete, fulfill, fill (up), carry out
_____	1) make, create, construct; 2) do, perform, make, cause to be, do with, claim, prepare, give, gain, celebrate, hold, exercise, evaluate, consider, show, spend, work
_____	1) keep, have on hand, watch, put/keep under guard; 2) keep, observe

Parsing

Inflected	Case/Person	Num	Gender/Tense	Voice	Mood	Lexical Form	Gloss
1. ἀγαπᾶτε							
2. βλέπεις							
3. ἀκούουσιν							
4. Πιστεύετε							
5. χαρᾶς							
6. πλεῖον							
7. δαιμονίοις							
8. ζητεῖ							
9. ποιέω							
10. τηροῦμεν							
11. ἀγαθοῦ							
12. λέγεις							
13. νόμον							
14. ποιοῦμεν							
15. ἔχουσιν							

16. ἔχεις							
17. λύει							
18. πρόσωπα							
19. λαλεῖς							
20. πιστεύομεν							

Translation

1. πάλιν ἀπέστειλεν (he sent) ἄλλους δούλους πλείονας τῶν πρώτων…[101]

2. ὁ δὲ Ἰησοῦς εἶπεν αὐτῷ, Τί με λέγεις ἀγαθόν; οὐδεὶς ἀγαθὸς εἰ μὴ εἷς ὁ θεός.[102]

3. ὅτι βλέποντες (seeing) οὐ βλέπουσιν καὶ ἀκούοντες (hearing) οὐκ ἀκούουσιν οὐδὲ συνίουσιν (do they understand)·[103]

4. οὗτός ἐστιν ὁ τὸν λόγον ἀκούων (hears) καὶ εὐθὺς μετὰ χαρᾶς λαμβάνων (receives) αὐτόν·[104]

5. εἰ δὲ πνεύματι ἄγεσθε (you are led), οὐκ ἐστὲ ὑπὸ νόμον.[105]

---

[101] Mt 21:36.
[102] Mk 10:18. Note the KJV rendering.
[103] Mt 13:13.
[104] Mt 13:20b. Be careful not to uncritically insert androcentric language at the beginning of this verse.
[105] Gal 5:18.

6. Εἶπεν δὲ πρὸς αὐτούς, Πῶς λέγουσιν τὸν Χριστὸν εἶναι Δαυὶδ υἱόν;[106]

7. …καὶ ποιεῖ τὴν γῆν καὶ τοὺς ἐν αὐτῇ κατοικοῦντας (the ones dwelling) ἵνα προσκυνήσουσιν (worship) τὸ θηρίον (beast) τὸ πρῶτον…[107]

8. καὶ ἀναστενάξας (sighing deeply) τῷ πνεύματι αὐτοῦ λέγει, Τί ἡ γενεὰ αὕτη ζητεῖ σημεῖον; ἀμὴν λέγω ὑμῖν, εἰ δοθήσεται (will be given) τῇ γενεᾷ ταύτῃ σημεῖον.[108]

---

[106] Lk 20:41.
[107] Rev 13:12.
[108] Mk 8:12. See *CL,* 109 (definition 1.a.α). Cf. Heb 3:11.

8

Present Middle/Passive Indicative and Contract Verbs

8.1 The Challenge of the Middle Voice

1. What is the major difference between the active and middle voice?
   _____
   _____

2. English has a middle voice. True or False
3. Most present and imperfect middle indicative verbs in the NT do not have an active form, so they're lexical form appears passive. True or False
4. Such "deponent" verbs can often be rendered as active in meaning but passive in form. True or False
5. Some scholars dispute deponency as a category, and assert that their forms always match their meaning. True or False.

8.2 Present Middle Indicative

1. The Present Middle Indicative is an action that
   _____
   _____

2. *Table of Verb Tenses*

Tense	Aug/ Red	Tense stem	TF + CV	Endings	First singular

3. *Table of Verb Endings*

		Primary Endings	Secondary Endings
Active Voice	Singular		ἔλυον ν/α
			ἔλυες ς
			ἔλυε(ν) (ν)
	Plural		ἐλύομεν μεν
			ἐλύετε τε
			ἔλυον ν
Midd/Pass Voice	Singular		ἐλυόμην μην
			ἐλύου σο
			ἐλύετο το
	Plural		ἐλυόμεθα μεθα
			ἐλύεσθε σθε
			ἐλύοντο ντο

4. Paradigm of Present Middle Indicative

	Form	Gloss	CV	Ending
1st Sg	ἔρχομαι			
2nd Sg	ἔρχῃ			
3rd Sg	ἔρχεται			
1st Pl	ἐρχόμεθα			
2nd Pl	ἔρχεσθε			
3rd Pl	ἔρχονται			

8.3 Present Passive Indicative

1. The Present Middle Indicative is _____.

2. *Table of Verb Tenses*

Tense	Aug/Red	Tense stem	TF + CV	Endings	First singular

3. Paradigm of Present Passive Indicative

	Form	Gloss	CV	Ending
1st Sg	λύομαι			
2nd Sg	λύῃ			
3rd Sg	λύεται			
1st Pl	λυόμεθα			
2nd Pl	λύεσθε			
3rd Pl	λύονται			

8.4 Contraction and Contract Verbs

1. Contract verbs are verbs that end in _____.
2. List the first five of the **Ten Rules of Contraction:**

   1. _____
   2. _____
   3. _____
   4. _____
   5. _____

Vocabulary

ἀποκρίνομαι _____
δεῖ _____
δύναμαι _____
ἔρχομαι _____
νύξ, νυκτός, ἡ _____
ὅστις, ἥτις, ὅτι _____
πορεύομαι or πορεύω _____
συνάγω _____
τόπος, -ου, ὁ _____
ὡς _____
βασιλεύς, -έως, ὁ _____
γεννάω _____
ζάω and ζῶ _____
Ἰουδαία, -ας, ἡ _____
Ἰουδαῖος, -αία, -αῖον _____
Ἰσραήλ, ὁ _____
καρπός, -οῦ, ὁ _____
ὅλος, -η, -ον _____
προσκυνέω _____
αἴρω _____
ἀποκτείνω _____
ἀποστέλλω _____
βαπτίζω _____

_____ answer, reply, counter, rejoin
_____ king, (chief) ruler
_____ one must, one needs, as need requires, one ought
_____ be able
_____ 1) come, arrive; 2) go
_____ a) to father, beget, procreate; b) bear
_____ 1) adj. Judean/Jewish; 2) n. Judean, Jew
_____ Judea

_____ Israel
_____ 1) fruit; 2) fruit, produce, yield/gain
_____ night
_____ rel. pron. 1) anyone who, whoever, whatever; 2) who, which, namely one (those) who
_____ 1) go, make one's way, die; 2) conduct oneself, live, walk
_____ 1) gather; 2) take in as guest; 3) join in
_____ 1) place, space; 2) responsibility; 3) opportunity
_____ adv. 1) (just) as, (just) like, similar to, in the manner that/of, as (though) it were, as if, as; 2) as though, with the thought that, like; 3) how; 4) when, after, while, when, as long as, since, in order that, so that, about, nearly, close to
_____ 1-3) live
_____ all (of), whole, entire
_____ do obeisance, pay homage, worship
_____ 1) raise up, lift; 2) take away, remove, carry off, expel
_____ kill
_____ send, send away/out/off
_____ a) wash, purify; b) immerse, dip, plunge, wash, baptize

Parsing

Inflected	Case/Person	Num	Gender/Tense	Voice	Mood	Lexical Form	Gloss
1. νύξ							
2. δύναμαι							
3. τόπῳ							
4. πορεύεσθε							
5. ἐπαγγελίαι							
6. καρπῶν							
7. ἀποκρίνομαι							
8. οὗ							
9. ἔρχεται							
10. βασιλεῖς							
11. ὅστις							
12. μείζονας							
13. σημεῖον							
14. γεννᾶται							
15. μεγάλα							
16. ἐκείνην							
17. τούτῳ							
18. ζάω							
19. διδασκάλων							
20. συνάγω							

Translation

1. καὶ ἐὰν βασιλεία ἐφ' ἑαυτὴν μερισθῇ (divided), οὐ δύναται σταθῆναι (stand) ἡ βασιλεία ἐκείνη·[109] _____

_____

---

[109] Mk 3:24.

2. καὶ γὰρ ἐγὼ ἄνθρωπός εἰμι ὑπὸ ἐξουσίαν, ἔχων ὑπ' ἐμαυτὸν στρατιώτας (soldiers), καὶ λέγω τούτῳ, Πορεύθητι (go!), καὶ πορεύεται, καὶ ἄλλῳ, Ἔρχου (come!), καὶ ἔρχεται, καὶ τῷ δούλῳ μου, Ποίησον (do!) τοῦτο, καὶ ποιεῖ.[110]

3. λαβὼν (receiving) οὖν τὸ ψωμίον (morsel) ἐκεῖνος ἐξῆλθεν (he went out) εὐθύς· ἦν δὲ νύξ.[111]

4. ἀμὴν ἀμὴν λέγω ὑμῖν, ὁ πιστεύων (the one believing) εἰς ἐμὲ τὰ ἔργα ἃ ἐγὼ ποιῶ κἀκεῖνος (works) ποιήσει, καὶ μείζονα τούτων ποιήσει (he will do), ὅτι ἐγὼ πρὸς τὸν πατέρα πορεύομαι·[112]

5. εἶπεν δὲ Αβρααμ Εἶπα (I speak/thought) γάρ Ἄρα (surely/therefore) οὐκ ἔστιν θεοσέβεια (piety) ἐν τῷ τόπῳ τούτῳ, ἐμέ τε ἀποκτενοῦσιν (they will kill) ἕνεκεν (because/for the sake of) τῆς γυναικός μου.[113]

6. ὅστις δ' ἂν ἀρνήσηταί (denies) με ἔμπροσθεν (before/in the presence of) τῶν ἀνθρώπων, ἀρνήσομαι κἀγὼ αὐτὸν ἔμπροσθεν τοῦ πατρός μου τοῦ ἐν τοῖσ οὐρανοῖς.[114]

7. καὶ συναγαγὼν (gathering) πάντας τοὺς ἀρχιερεῖς καὶ γραμματεῖς τοῦ λαοῦ ἐπυνθάνετο (he inquired) παρ' αὐτῶν ποῦ ὁ Χριστὸς γεννᾶται.[115]

---

[110] Mt 8:9.
[111] Jn 13:30.
[112] Jn 14:12.
[113] Gen 20:11, LXX. Note the use of capitals indicating quotations. Note also how contemporary translations add "of God" (on the basis of the Hebrew text, which contains *Elohim*, אֱלֹהִים).
[114] Mt 10:33.
[115] Mt 2:4. How is the second τοῦ functioning?

8. καὶ τὰ δέκα κέρατα (horns) ἃ εἶδες (you saw) δέκα βασιλεῖς εἰσιν, οἵτινες[116] βασιλείαν οὔπω ἔλαβον (have not received), ἀλλὰ ἐξουσίαν ὡς βασιλεῖς μίαν ὥραν λαμβάνουσιν (they receive) μετὰ τοῦ θηρίου.[117]

9. Καὶ ἐπροφήτευσεν (were prophets) Αγγαιος ὁ προφήτης καὶ Ζαχαριας ὁ τοῦ Αδδω προφητείαν (prophesied) ἐπὶ τοὺς Ιουδαίους τοὺς ἐν Ιουδα καὶ Ιερουσαλημ ἐν ὀνόματι θεοῦ Ισραηλ ἐπ᾽ αὐτούς…[118]

10. ἄρα γε ἀπὸ τῶν καρπῶν αὐτῶν ἐπιγνώσεσθε (you will know) αὐτούς.[119]

11. ἀμὴν ἀμὴν λέγω ὑμῖν, οὐκ ἔστιν δοῦλος μείζων τοῦ κυρίου αὐτοῦ οὐδὲ ἀπόστολος μείζων τοῦ πέμψαντος[120] αὐτόν.[121]

12. Στέφανος δὲ πλήρης χάριτος καὶ δυνάμεως ἐποίει (was doing) τέρατα (wonders) καὶ σημεῖα μεγάλα ἐν τῷ λαῷ.[122]

13. καὶ εἶπεν, Τοῦτο ποιήσω (I will do)· καθελῶ (I will tear down) μου τὰς ἀποθήκας (barns) καὶ μείζονας οἰκοδομήσω (will build), καὶ συνάξω (I will store) ἐκεῖ πάντα τὸν σῖτον (grain) καὶ τὰ ἀγαθά μου,[123]

---

[116] ὅστις, ἥτις, ὅτι.
[117] Rev 17:12.
[118] Ezra 5:1, LXX.
[119] Mt 7:20.
[120] πέμπω. (Here, in this verse, it forms an aorist participle.)
[121] Jn 13:16.
[122] Acts 6:8.
[123] Lk 12:18.

14. ἐξανέστησαν (stood up) δέ τινες τῶν ἀπὸ τῆς αἱρέσεως (sect) τῶν Φαρισαίων πεπιστευκότες (who had believed), λέγοντες (saying) ὅτι δεῖ περιτέμνειν (circumcise) αὐτοὺς παραγγέλλειν (direct them) τε τηρεῖν (to observe) τὸν νόμον Μωϋσέως.[124]

Chapter Eight: Present Middle/Indicative and Contract Verbs

Random Review

1. Fill out the following pronoun table (English meanings):

1st Person		2nd Person	
ἐγώ		σύ	
μου (ἐμοῦ)		σου (σοῦ)	
μοι (ἐμοί)		σοι (σοί)	
με (ἐμέ)		σε (σέ)	
ἡμεῖς		ὑμεῖς	
ἡμῶν		ὑμῶν	
ἡμῖν		ὑμῖν	
ἡμᾶς		ὑμᾶς	

2. Fill out the *Table of Personal Pronouns*:

1st	2nd	3rd M	3rd F	3rd N

9

Imperfect Indicative and εἰμί

9.1 Imperfect Active Indicative

1. The Imperfect Active Indicative indicates _____.
2. The Imperfect tense uses the _____ endings, and thus has an augment.
3. Where does the augment go in compound verbs that begin with a preposition?
   _____

4. *Table of Verb Tenses*

Tense	Aug/ Red	Tense stem	TF + CV	Endings	First singular
Pres act		pres	o/ε	prim act	λύω
Pres mid/pas		pres	o/ε	prim mid/pas	λύομαι
Imperf mid/pas	ε	pres	o/ε	sec mid/pas	ἐλυόμην

Chapter Nine: Imperfect Indicative and εἰμί

5. Table of Verb Endings

		Primary Endings	Secondary Endings
Active Voice	Singular		
Active Voice	Plural		
Midd/Pass Voice	Singular		ἐλυόμην μην ἐλύου σο ἐλύετο το
Midd/Pass Voice	Plural		ἐλυόμεθα μεθα ἐλύεσθε σθε ἐλύοντο ντο

6. Paradigm of Imperfect Active Indicative

	Form	Gloss	CV	Ending
1st Sg	ἔλυον			
2nd Sg	ἔλυες			
3rd Sg	ἔλυε(ν)			
1st Pl	ἐλύομεν			
2nd Pl	ἐλύετε			
3rd Pl	ἔλυον			

9.2 Imperfect Middle/Passive Indicative

1. *Table of Verb Tenses*

Tense	Aug/ Red	Tense stem	TF + CV	Endings	First singular
Present act		pres	o/ε	prim act	λύω
Present mid/pas		pres	o/ε	prim mid/pas	λύομαι

2. *Table of Verb Endings*

		Primary Endings	Secondary Endings
Active Voice	Singular		
	Plural		
Midd/Pass Voice	Singular		
	Plural		

3. Paradigm of Imperfect Middle/Passive Indicative

	Form	Gloss	CV	Ending
1ˢᵗ Sg	ἐλυόμην			
2ⁿᵈ Sg	ἐλύου			
3ʳᵈ Sg	ἐλύετο			
1ˢᵗ Pl	ἐλυόμεθα			
2ⁿᵈ Pl	ἐλύεσθε			
3ʳᵈ Pl	ἐλύοντο			

9.3 εἰμί

1. Εἰμί is the Greek verb meaning _____.
2. Fill-in the following table:

	Form	Translation
1 sg	εἰμί	
2 sg	εἶ	
3 sg	ἐστί(ν)	
1 pl	ἐσμέν	
2 pl	ἐστέ	
3 pl	εἰσί(ν)	

3. Fill-in the *Table of εἰμί Verbs*:

	Imperfect	Present	Future	Subjunctive
1 sg			ἔσομαι	ὦ
2 sg			ἔσῃ	ἦς
3 sg			ἔσται	ἦ
1 pl			ἐσόμεθα	ὦμεν
2 pl			ἔσεσθε	ἦτε
3 pl			ἔσονται	ὦσι(ν)

Vocabulary

ἄρτος, -ου, ὁ
ἀκολουθέω
ἀποθνῄσκω
βάλλω
χρόνος, -ου, ὁ
διδάσκω
ἔτι
εἰσέρχομαι
ἐγείρω
ἐκβάλλω
ἐκεῖ
ἐπερωτάω
ἐρωτάω
ἐξέρχομαι
εὑρίσκω
Φαρισαῖος, -ου, ὁ
γῆ, γῆς, ἡ
γινώσκω
γίνομαι
γλῶσσα, -ης, ἡ

Chapter Nine: Imperfect Indicative and εἰμί

κρίνω _____
λαμβάνω _____
λαός, -οῦ, ὁ _____
μένω _____
ὁράω _____
οὔτε _____
περιπατέω _____
προσεύχομαι _____
προσέρχομαι _____
πῦρ, πυρός, τό _____
θέλω _____
σοφία, -ας, ἡ _____
στόμα, -ατος, τό _____
συναγωγή, -ῆς, ἡ _____
σῴζω _____

_____ 1) know, learn of, find out; 2) think, understand, comprehend, perceive, notice, realize, conclude; 3) make acquaintance, recognize; 4) have intercourse
_____ 1) tongue; 2) tongue, language; 3) tongue
_____ rise, raise; a) get up; b) awaken, rouse, raise, rise; c) rise, appear, go
_____ I cast out, send out
_____ 1) there; 2) thither, in that place
_____ 1) prefer, favor; 2) judge, pass judgment on, condemn, go to court (with), press charges; 3) judge, come to a decision, decide, consider
_____ people
_____ 1) remain, stay; 2) await, wait for
_____ 1) see, appear, visit, look; 2) see, perceive, see to it that, take care of, see to (it), tend to (it)
_____ wisdom
_____ mouth

	save, rescue
_____	1) follow; 2) accompany
_____	teach, instruct
_____	1) ask; 2) ask for, demand
_____	1) ask; 2) ask, request
_____	1) wish to have, desire, want; 2) wish, have in mind, want, be ready, maintain; 3) like
_____	1) go about, walk about/around, walk; 2) walk, live
_____	1) synagogue; 2) assembly, synagogue; 3) meeting
_____	Pharisee
_____	1-2) time
_____	die
_____	1) bread, loaf (of bread); 2) bread, food
_____	1) throw, sow, scatter, pour, spew/spit, drop; 2) put, apply, lay, swing, deposit; 3) break loose, rush
_____	1) earth; 2) people, humanity; 3) land, country, region, ground
_____	1) be born, be produced; 2) be made, be performed, be done; 3) come to be, become, take place, happen, occur, arise, be, belong (to), now, turn out to be, prove to be, be, be there, appear, come, arrive
_____	go/enter in/into
_____	go/come out/away
_____	adv. 1) still, yet, anymore, anylonger, already/right; 2) yet, still
_____	1) find, locate, come across, discover, turn out to be, obtain; 2) find
_____	1) act. take; 2) pass. receive, take, get, take (up)
_____	neither…nor
_____	a) go forward, come in, answer; b) go before; c) go ahead
_____	pray
_____	fire

Parsing

Inflected	Case/Person	Num	Gender/Tense	Voice	Mood	Lexical Form	Gloss
1. ἐγείρεται							
2. ἐκρινόμεθα							
3. λαοῖς							
4. περιεπάτεις							
5. ἐγίνωσκεν							
6. ἐσῴζοντο							
7. γλώσσῃ							
8. συναγωγαῖς							
9. ἀποθνῄσκομεν							
10. ἐπηρώτων							
11. ἔμενον							
12. ἐξήρχετο							
13. χρόνου							
14. ἐδίδασκεν							
15. ἤθελες							
16. πῦρ							
17. ἐλάμβανεσθε							
18. ἐγίνετο							
19. προσηύχετο							
20. γῆς							

Translation

1. ἰδὼν (saw) δὲ ὁ Φαρισαῖος ὁ καλέσας (invited) αὐτὸν εἶπεν ἐν ἑαυτῷ λέγων (saying), Οὗτος εἰ ἦν προφήτης, ἐγίνωσκεν ἂν τίς καὶ ποταπὴ (what kind of) ἡ γυνὴ ἥτις ἅπτεται (touching) αὐτοῦ, ὅτι ἁμαρτωλός (sinner) ἐστιν.[125]

2. ὁ γὰρ λαλῶν γλώσσῃ οὐκ ἀνθρώποις λαλεῖ (speaks) ἀλλὰ θεῷ, οὐδεὶς γὰρ ἀκούει, πνεύματι δὲ λαλεῖ μυστήρια·[126]

3. ἀπεκρίθησαν καὶ εἶπαν αὐτῷ, Μὴ καὶ σὺ ἐκ τῆς Γαλιλαίας εἶ; ἐραύνησον (search!) καὶ ἴδε ὅτι ἐκ τῆς Γαλιλαίας προφήτης οὐκ ἐγείρεται.[127]

4. εἰ δὲ ἑαυτοὺς διεκρίνομεν (we judged), οὐκ ἂν ἐκρινόμεθα.[128]

5. συνήχθησαν (were gathered together) γὰρ ἐπ' ἀληθείας ἐν τῇ πόλει ταύτῃ ἐπὶ τὸν ἅγιον παῖδά (servant) σου Ἰησοῦν ὃν ἔχρισας (you anointed), Ἡρῴδης τε καὶ Πόντιος Πιλᾶτος σὺν (with) ἔθνεσιν καὶ λαοῖς Ἰσραήλ,…[129]

6. οὗτοι δὲ προελθόντες (had gone ahead) ἔμενον ἡμᾶς ἐν Τρῳάδι (Troas).[130]

---

[125] Lk 7:39.
[126] 1 Cor 14:2.
[127] Jn 7:52.
[128] 1 Cor 11:31.
[129] Acts 4:27.
[130] Acts 20:5.

7. ...τοῦ κρασπέδου (fringe) τοῦ ἱματίου αὐτοῦ ἅψωνται (touch)· καὶ ὅσοι ἂν ἥψαντο (touched) αὐτοῦ ἐσῴζοντο.[131]

8. καὶ αὐτὸς ἐδίδασκεν ἐν ταῖς συναγωγαῖς αὐτῶν, δοξαζόμενος ὑπὸ πάντων.[132]

9. Καὶ περιῆγεν (was going) ἐν ὅλῃ τῇ Γαλιλαίᾳ, διδάσκων (teaching) ἐν ταῖς συναγωγαῖς αὐτῶν καὶ κηρύσσων (proclaiming) τὸ εὐαγγέλιον τῆς βασιλείας καὶ θεραπεύων (healing) πᾶσαν νόσον (diseases) καὶ πᾶσαν μαλακίαν (sickness) ἐν τῷ λαῷ.[133]

10. εἰ κατὰ ἄνθρωπον ἐθηριομάχησα (I fought with wild beasts) ἐν Ἐφέσῳ (Ephesus), τί μοι τὸ ὄφελοσ (profit, n.); εἰ νεκροὶ οὐκ ἐγείρονται, Φάγωμεν (let us eat) καὶ πίωμεν (let us drink), αὔριον (tomorrow) γὰρ ἀποθνῄσκομεν.[134]

11. ἐξήρχετο δὲ καὶ δαιμόνια ἀπὸ πολλῶν, κρ[αυγ]άζοντα (shouting) καὶ λέγοντα ὅτι Σὺ εἶ ὁ υἱὸς τοῦ θεοῦ. καὶ ἐπιτιμῶν (rebuking) οὐκ εἴα (was permitting) αὐτὰ λαλεῖν (to speak), ὅτι ᾔδεισαν (they knew) τὸν Χριστὸν αὐτὸν εἶναι.[135]

---

[131] Mk 6:56.
[132] Lk 4:15.
[133] Mt 4:23.
[134] 1 Cor 15:32.
[135] Lk 4:41.

12. ἐνίσχυσεν (grew strong) ὁ λιμὸς (famine) ἐν τῇ πόλει, καὶ οὐκ ἦσαν ἄρτοι τῷ λαῷ τῆς γῆς.[136] _____

13. ὅτε δὲ ἦλθεν (came) τὸ πλήρωμα τοῦ χρόνου, ἐξαπέστειλεν (sent forth) ὁ θεὸς τὸν υἱὸν αὐτοῦ, γενόμενον (born) ἐκ γυναικός, γενόμενον ὑπὸ νόμον...[137]

_____

_____

14. Ἐγίνετο δὲ πάσῃ ψυχῇ φόβος, πολλά τε τέρατα (wonders) καὶ σημεῖα διὰ τῶν ἀποστόλων ἐγίνετο.[138] _____

15. ὁ Φαρισαῖος σταθεὶς (stood) πρὸς ἑαυτὸν ταῦτα προσηύχετο, Ὁ θεός, εὐχαριστῶ σοι ὅτι οὐκ εἰμὶ ὥσπερ οἱ λοιποὶ (other) τῶν ἀνθρώπων...[139]

_____

_____

16. οὐδέπω (not yet) γὰρ ἦν ἐπ᾽ οὐδενὶ αὐτῶν ἐπιπεπτωκός (fallen), μόνον δὲ βεβαπτισμένοι (baptized) ὑπῆρχον[140] (were) εἰς τὸ ὄνομα τοῦ κυρίου Ἰησοῦ. τότε ἐπετίθεσαν (they began laying) τὰς χεῖρας ἐπ᾽ αὐτοὺς καὶ ἐλάμβανον πνεῦμα ἅγιον.[141]

_____

_____

_____

17. ἀμὴν ἀμὴν λέγω σοι, ὅτε ἦς νεώτερος (younger), ἐζώννυες (you used to gird) σεαυτὸν καὶ περιεπάτεις[142] ὅπου ἤθελες·[143] ὅταν δὲ γηράσῃς[144] (you grow old),

---

[136] 2 Kings 25:3, LXX.
[137] Gal 4:4.
[138] Acts 2:43.
[139] Lk 18:11.
[140] This is a rare (imperfect) form of "to be."
[141] Acts 8:16-17.
[142] You saw this word in parsing; it is an irregular imperfect form that imitates the primary endings.
[143] Do not confuse this familiar word for the popular aorist form of ἔρχομαι (ἦλθεν).
[144] This word is subjunctive, so it has no time dimension, only aspect (aorist in this case).

ἐκτενεῖς (you will stretch out) τὰς χεῖράς σου, καὶ ἄλλος σε ζώσει (will gird) καὶ οἴσει (bring) ὅπου οὐ θέλεις (you do not wish).[145]

18. καὶ κύριος ἔβρεξεν (rained) ἐπὶ Σοδομα καὶ Γομορρα θεῖον (brimstone) καὶ πῦρ παρὰ κυρίου ἐκ τοῦ οὐρανοῦ.[146]

---

[145] Jn 21:18.
[146] Gen 19:24, LXX.

10

Future Active/Middle Indicative and Stem/Root Changes

10.1-2 The Future Tense and Forms of the Future

1. The aspect of of the future tense:
    a. Is somewhat of a puzzle
    b. Is agreed upon by all scholars
    c. Should probably be rendered with a simple aspect
    d. Both A and C
2. The future tense utilizes both a tense formative *and* a connecting vowel. True or False
3. There are many forms of the future because of different:
    a. Stems
    b. Tense formatives
    c. Connecting vowels
    d. Words

Chapter Ten: Future Active/Middle and Stem/Root Changes

10.3 Future Active Indicative

1. The Future Active Indicative indicates _____.

2. *Table of Verb Tenses*

Tense	Aug/ Red	Tense stem	TF + CV	Endings	First singular
Present act		pres	o/ε	prim act	λύω
Present mid/pas		pres	o/ε	prim mid/pas	λύομαι
Imperfect act	ε	pres	o/ε	sec act	ἔλυον
Imperfect mid/pas	ε	pres	o/ε	sec mid/pas	ἐλυόμην
Future mid		fut act	σ/εσ + o/ε	prim mid/pas	πορεύσομαι, μενοῦμαι
Future pas		aor pas	θη/η + o/ε	prim mid/pas	λυθήσομαι, ἀποσταλήσομαι

3. Paradigm of Future Active Indicative

	Form	*Gloss*	*TF*	*CV*	*Ending*
1ˢᵗ Sg	λύσω				
2ⁿᵈ Sg	λύσεις				
3ʳᵈ Sg	λύσει				
1ˢᵗ Pl	λύσομεν				
2ⁿᵈ Pl	λύσετε				
3ʳᵈ Pl	λύσουσι(ν)				

4. Since the sigma tense formative in the future tense verb can contract with consonants, it is important to review these rules of contraction. Complete the following:
    a. γραφ + σ + ο + μεθα = _____
    b. εξέρχ + σ + ε + ετε = _____
5. Liquid verbs have a stem ending in _, _, _, and _.
6. Liquid verbs have a _____ in their tense formative.
7. Paradigm of Liquid Future Active Indicative

	Form	Gloss	TF	CV	Ending
1st Sg	μενῶ				
2nd Sg	μενεῖς				
3rd Sg	μενεῖ				
1st Pl	μενοῦμεν				
2nd Pl	μενεῖτε				
3rd Pl	μενοῦσι(ν)				

10.4 Future Middle Indicative

1. *Table of Verb Tenses*

Tense	Aug/ Red	Tense stem	TF + CV	Endings	First singular
Present act		pres	o/ε	prim act	λύω
Present mid/pas		pres	o/ε	prim mid/pas	λύομαι
Imperfect act	ε	pres	o/ε	sec act	ἔλυον
Imperfect mid/pas	ε	pres	o/ε	sec mid/pas	ἐλυόμην
Future pas		aor pas	θη/η + o/ε	prim mid/pas	λυθήσομαι ἀποσταλήσομαι

2. Paradigm of Future Middle Indicative

	Form	Gloss	TF	CV	Ending
1st Sg	πορεύσομαι				
2nd Sg	πορεύσῃ				
3rd Sg	πορεύσεται				
1st Pl	πορευσόμεθα				
2nd Pl	πορεύσεσθε				
3rd Pl	πορεύσονται				

3. Paradigm of Liquid Future Middle Indicative

	Form	Gloss	TF	CV	Ending
1st Sg	μενοῦμαι				
2nd Sg	μενῇ				
3rd Sg	μενεῖται				
1st Pl	μενούμεθα				
2nd Pl	μενεῖσθε				
3rd Pl	μενοῦνται				

10.5-6 Stem and Root Changes

1. There are _____ different tense stems in Greek verbs:

   a. _____

   b. _____

   c. _____

   d. _____

   e. _____

   f. _____

2. What are the most common patterns of stem changes?

   a. Removal of _____

   b. Removing an _____

   c. Removing an _____

3. Complete the *Table of Root Changes*:

Aorist	Present (Lex)	Future

4. Complete the *Table of εἰμί Verbs*

	Imperfect	Present	Future	Subjunctive
1 sg				ὦ
2 sg				ᾖς
3 sg				ᾖ
1 pl				ὦμεν
2 pl				ἦτε
3 pl				ὦσι(ν)

Vocabulary

ἀπέρχομαι
ἄρχω
γράφω
διό
δοξάζω
δύναμις, -εως, ἡ
κηρύσσω
πίνω
ἄγω
αἷμα, -ατος, τό
ἕκαστος, -η, -ον
ἱμάτιον, -ου, τό
ὄρος, ὄρους, τό
ὑπάγω
φοβέομαι
χαίρω
αἰτέω
μᾶλλον
μαρτυρέω

_____ 1) lead, bring, carry, take; 2) spend, hold; 3) to go
_____ 1) act. rule; 2) begin
_____ blood, human being
_____ ask, ask for, request
_____ go, go away/off, depart, leave
_____ 1) be happy/glad/delighted, rejoice; 2) greetings
_____ conj. therefore, for this reason
_____ glorify
_____ 1) power, might; 2) powerful/wondrous deed, miracle; 3) power
_____ each, every; n. each one, every one
_____ 1) be afraid, fear, be afraid of be apprehensive/worried about; 2) have deep respect (for); be filled with awe

_____ write, inscribe
_____ a) clothing, apparel; b) cloak, coat
_____ proclaim
_____ 1) (much) more, all the more, still more; 2) rather, instead
_____ testify, attest
_____ hill, mount, mountain
_____ drink
_____ a) go away, leave; b) go, be on one's way

Parsing

Inflected	Case/Person	Num	Gender/Tense	Voice	Mood	Lexical Form	Gloss
1. ἱμάτια							
2. πορεύσομαι							
3. πίνετε							
4. ἄξει							
5. ἤγεσθε							
6. ἐξελεύσονται							
7. χαῖρει							
8. ζητήσετέ							
9. γράψω							
10. αἰτήσουσιν							
11. δοξάζεται							
12. ὄψομαι							
13. χαρεῖται							
14. ὑπῆγον							
15. ποιήσουσιν							
16. πληρώσεις							
17. ὑπάγει							
18. αἷμα							
19. μαρτυρήσει							
20. κηρύσσεται							

Translation

1. ὁ δὲ θεός μου πληρώσει πᾶσαν χρείαν (needs, n.) ὑμῶν κατὰ τὸ πλοῦτος αὐτοῦ ἐν δόξῃ ἐν Χριστῷ Ἰησοῦ.[147] _____

2. καὶ ὑμεῖς οὖν νῦν μὲν λύπην (grief) ἔχετε· πάλιν δὲ ὄψομαι ὑμᾶς, καὶ χαρήσεται ὑμῶν ἡ καρδία, καὶ τὴν χαρὰν ὑμῶν οὐδεὶς αἴρει ἀφ' ὑμῶν.[148]

3. ἀποσυναγώγους (outcasts from the synonogue) ποιήσουσιν ὑμᾶς· ἀλλ' ἔρχεται ὥρα ἵνα πᾶς ὁ ἀποκτείνας[149] ὑμᾶς δόξῃ (think) λατρείαν (service) προσφέρειν (bring) τῷ θεῷ.[150] καὶ ταῦτα ποιήσουσιν ὅτι οὐκ ἔγνωσαν (they have not known) τὸν πατέρα οὐδὲ ἐμέ.[151]

4. ἐμβλέψατε (look!) εἰς τὰ πετεινὰ (birds) τοῦ οὐρανοῦ ὅτι οὐ σπείρουσιν (sow) οὐδὲ θερίζουσιν (reap) οὐδὲ συνάγουσιν (gather) εἰς ἀποθήκας (barns), καὶ ὁ πατὴρ ὑμῶν ὁ οὐράνιος[152] τρέφει (feeds) αὐτά· οὐχ ὑμεῖς μᾶλλον διαφέρετε (you worth) αὐτῶν;[153]

---

[147] Php 4:19.
[148] Jn 16:22.
[149] Participle (aor, act, sg, nom, masc).
[150] This last phrase is very difficult to render in English. You may need to supply "they" as the subject of "bring."
[151] Jn 16:2-3.
[152] This is an adj., not a noun.
[153] Mt 6:26.

5. Ὅταν ἔλθῃ[154] ὁ παράκλητος ὃν ἐγὼ πέμψω (I will send) ὑμῖν παρὰ τοῦ πατρός, τὸ πνεῦμα τῆς ἀληθείας ὃ παρὰ τοῦ πατρὸς ἐκπορεύεται (proceeds), ἐκεῖνος μαρτυρήσει περὶ ἐμοῦ·[155]

    _____
    _____
    _____
    _____

6. καὶ ἔσονται ὡς μαχηταὶ (warriors) τοῦ Εφραιμ, καὶ χαρήσεται ἡ καρδία αὐτῶν ὡς ἐν οἴνῳ, καὶ τὰ τέκνα αὐτῶν ὄψονται καὶ εὐφρανθήσονται (shall rejoice), καὶ χαρεῖται ἡ καρδία αὐτῶν ἐπὶ τῷ κυρίῳ.[156]

    _____
    _____
    _____
    _____

7. ζητήσετέ με καὶ οὐχ εὑρήσετέ *με*, καὶ ὅπου εἰμὶ ἐγὼ ὑμεῖς οὐ δύνασθε ἐλθεῖν (to come).[157] _____

8. Μὴ χαῖρε, Ισραηλ, μηδὲ εὐφραίνου (exult) καθὼς οἱ λαοί[158], διότι ἐπόρνευσας ἀπὸ τοῦ θεοῦ σου.[159] _____
    _____

9. ...ὥστε θαρροῦντας ἡμᾶς λέγειν,
    Κύριος ἐμοὶ βοηθός (helper),
        [καὶ] οὐ φοβηθήσομαι,
    τί ποιήσει μοι ἄνθρωπος;[160] _____
    _____

10. καὶ ἔσται εἰς εὐφροσύνην (gladness) καὶ εἰς αἴνεσιν (praise) καὶ εἰς μεγαλειότητα (greatness) παντὶ τῷ λαῷ τῆς γῆς, οἵτινες ἀκούσονται πάντα τὰ ἀγαθά, ἃ ἐγὼ

---

[154] Subj. of ἔρχομαι.
[155] Jn 15:26.
[156] Zech 10:7, LXX
[157] Jn 7:34. Don't forget to consult Comfort regarding the textual variant in this verse.
[158] This term is in the nominative and remains the subject somehow.
[159] Hos 9:1, LXX.
[160] Heb 13:6.

ποιήσω, καὶ φοβηθήσονται καὶ πικρανθήσονται (be embittered) περὶ πάντων τῶν ἀγαθῶν καὶ περὶ πάσης τῆς εἰρήνης, ἧς ἐγὼ ποιήσω αὐτοῖς.[161]

_____

11. ἀντιτασσομένων (they resisted) δὲ αὐτῶν καὶ βλασφημούντων (blasphemed) ἐκτιναξάμενος (he shook) τὰ ἱμάτια εἶπεν πρὸς αὐτούς, Τὸ αἷμα ὑμῶν ἐπὶ τὴν κεφαλὴν ὑμῶν· καθαρὸς (am clean) ἐγώ· ἀπὸ τοῦ νῦν εἰς τὰ ἔθνη πορεύσομαι.[162]

_____

12. εἴτε οὖν ἐσθίετε (you eat) εἴτε πίνετε εἴτε τι ποιεῖτε, πάντα εἰς δόξαν θεοῦ ποιεῖτε.[163]

13. Εἰ δὲ Χριστὸς κηρύσσεται ὅτι ἐκ νεκρῶν ἐγήγερται (has been raised), πῶς λέγουσιν ἐν ὑμῖν τινες ὅτι ἀνάστασις (resurrection) νεκρῶν οὐκ ἔστιν; εἰ δὲ ἀνάστασις νεκρῶν οὐκ ἔστιν, οὐδὲ Χριστὸς ἐγήγερται· εἰ δὲ Χριστὸς οὐκ ἐγήγερται, κενὸν (vain) ἄρα (then) καὶ τὸ κήρυγμα ἡμῶν, κενὴ καὶ ἡ πίστις ὑμῶν,[164]

_____

[161] Jer 33:9. LXX (40:9).
[162] Acts 18:6. The phrase "ἀπὸ τοῦ νῦν" is something of an idiom; in English we'd say "from now *on*" (not "from the now").
[163] 1 Cor 10:31.
[164] 1 Cor 15:12-14.

14. εἰ γὰρ πιστεύομεν ὅτι Ἰησοῦς ἀπέθανεν (died) καὶ ἀνέστη (rose again), οὕτως καὶ ὁ θεὸς τοὺς κοιμηθέντας (those who have fallen asleep) διὰ τοῦ Ἰησοῦ ἄξει σὺν αὐτῷ.[165] _____

15. Οἴδατε ὅτι ὅτε ἔθνη (pagans) ἦτε (you were) πρὸς τὰ εἴδωλα (idols) τὰ ἄφωνα (mute) ὡς ἂν ἤγεσθε ἀπαγόμενοι.[166] _____

16. καὶ γράψω ἐπ' αὐτὸν τὸ ὄνομα τοῦ θεοῦ μου καὶ τὸ ὄνομα τῆς πόλεως τοῦ θεοῦ μου, τῆς καινῆς Ἰερουσαλήμ, ἡ καταβαίνουσα (comes down) ἐκ τοῦ οὐρανοῦ ἀπὸ τοῦ θεοῦ μου, καὶ τὸ ὄνομά μου τὸ καινόν (new).[167] _____

---

[165] 1 Thess 4:14.
[166] 1 Cor 12:2. Compare and contrast how the NRSV, NIV, and NASB chose to render "ὡς ἂν ἤγεσθε."
[167] Rev 3:12.

11

Future Passive and Aorist

11.1 The Future Passive Tense

1. The future passive tense is different from the other future tenses because it has the _____ tense stem.
2. Instead of "liquid" verbs with a specific tense formative, the future passive simply uses two different tense formatives regardless of whether the word is a liquid or not. True or False
3. *Table of Verb Tenses*

Tense	Aug/ Red	Tense stem	TF + CV	Endings	First singular
Present act		pres	o/ε	prim act	λύω
Present mid/pas		pres	o/ε	prim mid/pas	λύομαι
Imperfect act	ε	pres	o/ε	sec act	ἔλυον
Imperfect mid/pas	ε	pres	o/ε	sec mid/pas	ἐλυόμην

4. Paradigm of 1st Future Passive Indicative

	Form	Gloss	TF	CV	Ending
1st Sg	λυθήσομαι				
2nd Sg	λυθήσῃ				
3rd Sg	λυθήσεται				
1st Pl	λυθησόμεθα				
2nd Pl	λυθήσεσθε				
3rd Pl	λυθήσονται				

5. Paradigm of 2nd Future Passive Indicative

	Form	Gloss	TF	CV	Ending
1st Sg	ἀποσταλήσομαι				
2nd Sg	ἀποσταλήσῃ				
3rd Sg	ἀποσταλήσεται				
1st Pl	ἀποσταλησόμεθα				
2nd Pl	ἀποσταλήσεσθε				
3rd Pl	ἀποσταλήσονται				

11.3-4 Aorist and Aorist Active Indicative

1. The Aorist tense indicates a _____ action occurring in the ____.
2. *Table of Verb Tenses*

Tense	Aug/ Red	Tense stem	TF + CV	Endings	First singular
Present act		pres	o/ε	prim act	λύω
Present mid/pas		pres	o/ε	prim mid/pas	λύομαι
Imperfect act	ε	pres	o/ε	sec act	ἔλυον
Imperfect mid/pas	ε	pres	o/ε	sec mid/pas	ἐλυόμην
Future act		fut act	σ/εσ + o/ε	prim act	λύσω μενῶ
Future mid		fut act	σ/εσ + o/ε	prim mid/pas	πορεύσομαι μενοῦμαι
Future pas		aor pas	θησ/ησ + o/ε	prim mid/pas	λυθήσομαι ἀποσταλήσομαι
Aorist mid	ε	aor act	σα / o/ε	sec mid/pas	ἐλυσάμην ἐγενόμην
Aorist pas	ε	aor pas	θη/η	sec act	ἐλύθην ἐγράφην

3. Paradigm of 1st Aorist Active Indicative

	Form	Gloss	TF	CV	Ending
1st Sg	ἔλυσα				
2nd Sg	ἔλυσας				
3rd Sg	ἔλυσε(ν)				
1st Pl	ἐλύσαμεν				
2nd Pl	ἐλύσατε				
3rd Pl	ἔλυσαν				

4. Paradigm of Liquid Aorist Active Indicative

	Form	Gloss	TF	CV	Ending
1st Sg	ἔμεινα				
2nd Sg	ἔμεινας				
3rd Sg	ἔμεινε(ν)				
1st Pl	ἐμείναμεν				
2nd Pl	ἐμείνατε				
3rd Pl	ἔμειναν				

5. Paradigm of 2nd Aorist Active Indicative

	Form	Gloss	TF	CV	Ending
1st Sg	ἔλαβον				
2nd Sg	ἔλαβες				
3rd Sg	ἔλαβε(ν)				
1st Pl	ἐλάβομεν				
2nd Pl	ἐλάβετε				
3rd Pl	ἔλαβον				

11.5 Aorist Middle Indicative

1. *Table of Verb Tenses*

Tense	Aug/Red	Tense stem	TF + CV	Endings	First singular
Present act		pres	o/ε	prim act	λύω
Present mid/pas		pres	o/ε	prim mid/pas	λύομαι
Imperfect act	ε	pres	o/ε	sec act	ἔλυον
Imperfect mid/pas	ε	pres	o/ε	sec mid/pas	ἐλυόμην
Future act		fut act	σ/εσ + o/ε	prim act	λύσω μενῶ
Future mid		fut act	σ/εσ + o/ε	prim mid/pas	πορεύσομαι μενοῦμαι
Future pas		aor pas	θησ/ησ + o/ε	prim mid/pas	λυθήσομαι ἀποσταλήσομαι
Aorist pas	ε	aor pas	θη/η	sec act	ἐλύθην ἐγράφην

2. Paradigm of 1st Aorist Middle Indicative

	Form	Gloss	TF	CV	Ending
1st Sg	ἐλυσάμην				
2nd Sg	ἐλύσω				
3rd Sg	ἐλύσατο				
1st Pl	ἐλυσάμεθα				
2nd Pl	ἐλύσασθε				
3rd Pl	ἐλύσαντο				

3. Paradigm of 2nd Aorist Middle Indicative

	Form	Gloss	TF	CV	Ending
1st Sg	ἐγενόμην				
2nd Sg	ἐγένου				
3rd Sg	ἐγένετο				
1st Pl	ἐγενόμεθα				
2nd Pl	ἐγένεσθε				
3rd Pl	ἐγένοντο				

11.6 Aorist Passive Indicative

1. *Table of Verb Tenses*

Tense	Aug/Red	Tense stem	TF + CV	Endings	First singular
Present act		pres	o/ε	prim act	λύω
Present mid/pas		pres	o/ε	prim mid/pas	λύομαι
Imperfect act	ε	pres	o/ε	sec act	ἔλυον
Imperfect mid/pas	ε	pres	o/ε	sec mid/pas	ἐλυόμην
Future act		fut act	σ/εσ + o/ε	prim act	λύσω μενῶ
Future mid		fut act	σ/εσ + o/ε	prim mid/pas	πορεύσομαι μενοῦμαι
Future pas		aor pas	θησ/ησ + o/ε	prim mid/pas	λυθήσομαι ἀποσταλήσομαι

2. Paradigm of 1st Aorist Passive Indicative

	Form	Gloss	TF	CV	Ending
1st Sg	ἐλύθην				
2nd Sg	ἐλύθης				
3rd Sg	ἐλύθη				
1st Pl	ἐλύθημεν				
2nd Pl	ἐλύθητε				
3rd Pl	ἐλύθησαν				

3. Paradigm of 2nd Aorist Passive Indicative

	Form	Gloss	TF	CV	Ending
1st Sg	ἐγράφην				
2nd Sg	ἐγράφης				
3rd Sg	ἐγράφη				
1st Pl	ἐγράφημεν				
2nd Pl	ἐγράφητε				
3rd Pl	ἐγράφησαν				

Vocabulary

ἀναβαίνω _____
καταβαίνω _____
δεξιός, -ιά, -ιόν _____
δύο _____
ἕτερος, -α, -ον _____
εὐαγγελίζω _____
θεωρέω _____
κάθημαι _____
ἀρχιερεύς, -έως, ὁ _____
παρακαλέω _____
πείθω _____
τρεῖς, τρία _____
ἀσπάζομαι _____
γραμματεύς, -έως, ὁ _____
ἱερόν, -οῦ, τό _____
κράζω _____
οὐχι _____
παιδίον, -ου, τό _____
σπείρω _____
δέχομαι _____
δοκέω _____
ἐσθίω _____
πέμπω _____
φέρω _____

_____ go up
_____ 1) high priest, chief priest; 2) chief priests
_____ 1) greet, say good-bye to, say farewell
_____ receive
_____ right
_____ 1) think, opine, regard/recognize, decide, resolve; 2) seem (good)

Chapter Eleven: Future Passive and Aorist

_____	two
_____	1) other, another; 2) other, another, different
_____	1) eat; 2) eat, devour, consume
_____	1) bring/announce good news; 2) publish good news/tidings, publish the good news, publish the gospel
_____	1) bring, conduct; 2) bear, bring, direct, establish; 3) bear; 4) bear, produce
_____	1) secretary (of state), clerk; 2) legal scholar, teacher of the law
_____	sanctuary, temple
_____	come/go down
_____	sit (down), take a seat
_____	1) scream, cry out; 2) call out
_____	not, no
_____	child, infant
_____	1) invite, entreat, implore; 2) comfort, console; 3) urge, exhort, encourage, say something friendly
_____	a) persuade, convince, win over, please, assure, reassure; b) be persuaded/convinced, be certain, submit (to), comply, conform to; c) have confidence
_____	send
_____	1) look at, observe, watch, behold, Catch sight of, take notice of; 2) infer, see, perceive, experience
_____	sow seed
_____	three

Parsing

Inflected	Case/Person	Num	Gender/Tense	Voice	Mood	Lexical Form	Gloss
1. ἠσπάσατο							
2. ἀναβαίνει							
3. παρακληθήσεσθε							
4. εὐηγγελισάμην							
5. ἐξῆλθεν							
6. ἔπεισαν							
7. Λαμβάνομεν							
8. ἔπεμψα							
9. ἐκάθισαν							
10. ἀρχιερεῖς							
11. φάγεται							
12. θέλετε							
13. ἠνέχθη							
14. γραμματεῖς							
15. ἔδοξε							
16. σπείρεται							
17. σωθήσομαι							
18. δεξιά							
19. ἐποίησεν							

Translation

1. Γνωρίζω (I make known/remind) δὲ ὑμῖν, ἀδελφοί, τὸ εὐαγγέλιον ὃ εὐηγγελισάμην ὑμῖν, ὃ καὶ παρελάβετε,[168] _____

2. Καὶ ἔρχονται πάλιν εἰς Ἱεροσόλυμα. καὶ ἐν τῷ ἱερῷ περιπατοῦντος αὐτοῦ ἔρχονται πρὸς αὐτὸν οἱ ἀρχιερεῖς καὶ οἱ γραμματεῖς[169] καὶ οἱ πρεσβύτεροι, καὶ ἔλεγον[170] αὐτῷ, Ἐν ποίᾳ ἐξουσίᾳ ταῦτα ποιεῖς; ἢ τίς σοι ἔδωκεν τὴν ἐξουσίαν ταύτην ἵνα ταῦτα ποιῇσ[171];[172]

3. ...ἔλεγεν γὰρ ἐν ἑαυτῇ, Ἐὰν μόνον ἅψωμαι (I touch) τοῦ ἱματίου αὐτοῦ σωθήσομαι. ὁ δὲ Ἰησοῦς στραφεὶς (turning) καὶ ἰδὼν αὐτὴν εἶπεν, Θάρσει (take courage), θύγατερ (daughter)· ἡ πίστις σου σέσωκέν σε. καὶ ἐσώθη ἡ γυνὴ ἀπὸ τῆς ὥρας ἐκείνης.[173]

4. καὶ ἰδοὺ ἔκραξαν λέγοντες, Τί ἡμῖν καὶ σοί,[174] υἱὲ[175] τοῦ θεοῦ; ἦλθες ὧδε πρὸ καιροῦ βασανίσαι (to torment) ἡμᾶς;[176]

---

[168] 1 Cor 15:1a.
[169] What case are these two words in? Notice the articles carefully, and double-check these words in the parsing above.
[170] Pay attention to the tense of this common word and how it should be translated.
[171] Subjunctive.
[172] Mk 11:27-28.
[173] Mt 9:21-22. Is the NASB rendering of the last phrase good or not so much?
[174] This is a difficult phrase and can be captured in a number of ways.
[175] This is one of the rare uses of the vocative case, "the case of direct address." See *A Concise Greek Grammar*, 2.1.
[176] Mt 8:29.

5. Ἐγὼ Ἰησοῦς ἔπεμψα τὸν ἄγγελόν μου μαρτυρῆσαι[177] ὑμῖν ταῦτα ἐπὶ ταῖς ἐκκλησίαις. ἐγώ εἰμι ἡ ῥίζα (root) καὶ τὸ γένος Δαυίδ, ὁ ἀστὴρ ὁ λαμπρὸς (bright) ὁ πρωϊνός (morning).[178]

6. Σπείρεται (it is sown) ἐν ἀτιμίᾳ (dishonor), ἐγείρεται ἐν δόξῃ· σπείρεται ἐν ἀσθενείᾳ (weakness), ἐγείρεται ἐν δυνάμει· σπείρεται σῶμα ψυχικόν, ἐγείρεται σῶμα πνευματικόν. εἰ ἔστιν σῶμα ψυχικόν, ἔστιν καὶ πνευματικόν.[179]

7. εὐθὺς κράξας ὁ πατὴρ τοῦ παιδίου ἔλεγεν, Πιστεύω· βοήθει (help!) μου τῇ ἀπιστίᾳ (unbelief). ἰδὼν δὲ ὁ Ἰησοῦς ὅτι ἐπισυντρέχει (was quickly gathering) ὄχλος, ἐπετίμησεν (he rebuked) τῷ πνεύματι τῷ ἀκαθάρτῳ (unclean) λέγων (saying) αὐτῷ, Τὸ ἄλαλον (deaf) καὶ κωφὸν (mute) πνεῦμα, ἐγὼ ἐπιτάσσω (I command you) σοι, ἔξελθε[180] ἐξ αὐτοῦ καὶ μηκέτι εἰσέλθῃς εἰς αὐτόν. καὶ κράξας καὶ πολλὰ σπαράξας (greatly convulsing) ἐξῆλθεν· καὶ ἐγένετο ὡσεὶ (as) νεκρός, ὥστε τοὺς πολλοὺς λέγειν[181] ὅτι ἀπέθανεν.[182]

---

[177] Infinitive.
[178] Rev 22:16.
[179] 1 Cor 15:43-44.
[180] Imperative.
[181] Infinitive.
[182] Mk 9:24-27.

8. Τότε ἔδοξε τοῖς ἀποστόλοις καὶ τοῖς πρεσβυτέροις σὺν ὅλῃ τῇ ἐκκλησίᾳ ἐκλεξαμένους (to choose) ἄνδρας ἐξ αὐτῶν πέμψαι[183] εἰς Ἀντιόχειαν σὺν τῷ Παύλῳ καὶ Βαρναβᾷ, Ἰούδαν τὸν καλούμενον (called) Βαρσαββᾶν καὶ Σιλᾶν, ἄνδρας ἡγουμένους (leading) ἐν τοῖς ἀδελφοῖς,[184]

9. παραγενόμενοι (when they arrived) δὲ εἰς Ἰερουσαλὴμ παρεδέχθησαν ἀπὸ τῆς ἐκκλησίας καὶ τῶν ἀποστόλων καὶ τῶν πρεσβυτέρων, ἀνήγγειλάν (they reported) τε ὅσα ὁ θεὸς ἐποίησεν μετ' αὐτῶν.[185]

10. ὡς εἴ τινα μήτηρ παρακαλέσει, οὕτως καὶ ἐγὼ παρακαλέσω ὑμᾶς, καὶ ἐν Ἰερουσαλημ παρακληθήσεσθε.[186]

11. ὅτι τρεῖς εἰσιν οἱ μαρτυροῦντες,[187] τὸ πνεῦμα καὶ τὸ ὕδωρ καὶ τὸ αἷμα, καὶ οἱ τρεῖς εἰς τὸ ἕν εἰσιν. εἰ τὴν μαρτυρίαν τῶν ἀνθρώπων λαμβάνομεν, ἡ μαρτυρία τοῦ θεοῦ

---

[183] Infinitive.
[184] Acts 15:22.
[185] Acts 15:4.
[186] Is 66:13, LXX.
[187] Participle.

μείζων ἐστίν, ὅτι αὕτη ἐστὶν ἡ μαρτυρία τοῦ θεοῦ, ὅτι μεμαρτύρηκεν[188] περὶ τοῦ υἱοῦ αὐτοῦ. [189]

___

12. Οἱ δὲ ἀρχιερεῖς καὶ οἱ πρεσβύτεροι ἔπεισαν τοὺς ὄχλους ἵνα αἰτήσωνται (to ask) τὸν Βαραββᾶν, τὸν δὲ Ἰησοῦν ἀπολέσωσιν (to put to death). ἀποκριθεὶς (answered) δὲ ὁ ἡγεμὼν (governor) εἶπεν αὐτοῖς, Τίνα θέλετε ἀπὸ τῶν δύο ἀπολύσω (to release) ὑμῖν; οἱ δὲ εἶπαν, Τὸν Βαραββᾶν.[190]

___

13. καὶ ἠνέχθη ἡ κεφαλὴ αὐτοῦ ἐπὶ πίνακι (platter) καὶ ἐδόθη (given) τῷ κορασίῳ (to the girl), καὶ ἤνεγκεν τῇ μητρὶ αὐτῆς.[191]

___

14. Καὶ σὺν αὐτῷ σταυροῦσιν (crucified) δύο λῃστάς (robbers), ἕνα ἐκ δεξιῶν καὶ ἕνα ἐξ εὐωνύμων (left) αὐτοῦ.[192]

___

15. Ἀναστᾶσα (arose) δὲ Μαριὰμ ἐν ταῖς ἡμέραις ταύταις ἐπορεύθη (travelled) εἰς τὴν ὀρεινὴν μετὰ σπουδῆς εἰς πόλιν Ἰούδα, καὶ εἰσῆλθεν εἰς τὸν οἶκον Ζαχαρίου καὶ ἠσπάσατο τὴν Ἐλισάβετ.[193]

___

[188] Perfect tense. (Next chapter).
[189] 1 Jn 5:7-8. This is the "Comma Johanneum," and has a notorious variant in the KJV ("Father, word, and Holy Ghost…").
[190] Mt 27:20-21.
[191] Mt 14:11.
[192] Mk 15:27.
[193] Lk 1:39-40.

16. Καὶ εἶδον θρόνους καὶ ἐκάθισαν ἐπ' αὐτοὺς καὶ κρίμα ἐδόθη (was given) αὐτοῖς, καὶ τὰς ψυχὰς τῶν πεπελεκισμένων (of those who had been beheaded) διὰ τὴν μαρτυρίαν Ἰησοῦ καὶ διὰ τὸν λόγον τοῦ θεοῦ,[194]

---

[194] Rev 20:4a.

12

Perfect and PluPerfect

12.1 Perfect Indicative

1. The perfect tense uses the completive aspect, which reflects _____ _____.

2. The perfect tense can involve _____ or _____ time, but is usually translated as _____ time in a way that affects the speaker's _____ circumstances.

3. The perfect tense stem undergoes reduplication.

4. Reduplicate the following stems:

    a. Λέγω → _____
    b. Θεωρεω → _____
    c. ἄγω → _____
    d. ἔρχομαι → _____
    e. δύναμαι → _____
    f. καλέω → _____
    g. βάλλω → _____
    h. εκβάλλω → _____
    i. ἀπέρχομαι → _____

12.2 Perfect Active Indicative

1. *Table of Verb Tenses*

Tense	Aug/Red	Tense stem	TF + CV	Endings	First singular
Present act		pres	ο/ε	prim act	λύω
Present mid/pas		pres	ο/ε	prim mid/pas	λύομαι
Imperfect act	ε	pres	ο/ε	sec act	ἔλυον
Imperfect mid/pas	ε	pres	ο/ε	sec mid/pas	ἐλυόμην
Future act		fut act	σ/εσ + ο/ε	prim act	λύσω μενῶ
Future mid		fut act	σ/εσ + ο/ε	prim mid/pas	πορεύσομαι μενοῦμαι
Future pas		aor pas	θησ/ησ + ο/ε	prim mid/pas	λυθήσομαι ἀποσταλήσομαι
Aorist act	ε	aor act	σα/α / ο/ε	sec act	ἔλυσα ἔμεινα ἔλαβον
Aorist mid	ε	aor act	σα / ο/ε	sec mid/pas	ἐλυσάμην ἐγενόμην
Aorist pas	ε	aor pas	θη/η	sec act	ἐλύθην ἐγράφην
Perfect mid/pas	λε			prim mid/pas	λέλυμαι
Pluperf act	[ε]λε	perf act	κ / ει	sec act	[ἐ]λελύκειν [ἐ]γεγράφειν
Pluperf mid/pas	[ε]λε	perf pas		sec pas	[ἐ]λελύμην

2. Paradigm of Perfect Active Indicative

	Form	Gloss	Ending
1st Sg	λέλυκα		
2nd Sg	λέλυκας		
3rd Sg	λέλυκε(ν)		
1st Pl	λελύκαμεν		
2nd Pl	λελύκατε		
3rd Pl	λελύκασι(ν)		

12.3 Perfect Middle-Passive Indicative

1. Table of Verb Tenses

Tense	Aug/Red	Tense stem	TF + CV	Endings	First singular
Present act		pres	o/ε	prim act	λύω
Present mid/pas		pres	o/ε	prim mid/pas	λύομαι
Imperfect act	ε	pres	o/ε	sec act	ἔλυον
Imperfect mid/pas	ε	pres	o/ε	sec mid/pas	ἐλυόμην
Future act		fut act	σ/εσ + o/ε	prim act	λύσω μενῶ
Future mid		fut act	σ/εσ + o/ε	prim mid/pas	πορεύσομαι μενοῦμαι
Future pas		aor pas	θησ/ησ + o/ε	prim mid/pas	λυθήσομαι ἀποσταλήσομαι
Aorist act	ε	aor act	σα/α / o/ε	sec act	ἔλυσα ἔμεινα ἔλαβον
Aorist mid	ε	aor act	σα / o/ε	sec mid/pas	ἐλυσάμην ἐγενόμην
Aorist pas	ε	aor pas	θη/η	sec act	ἐλύθην ἐγράφην

Pluperf act	[ε]λε perf act	κ / ει sec act	[ε]λελύκειν
			[ε]γεγράφειν
Pluperf mid/pas	[ε]λε perf pas	sec pas	[ε]λελύμην

2. Paradigm of Perfect Middle/Passive Active Indicative

	Form	Gloss	Ending
1ˢᵗ Sg	λέλυμαι		
2ⁿᵈ Sg	λέλυσαι		
3ʳᵈ Sg	λέλυται		
1ˢᵗ Pl	λελύμεθα		
2ⁿᵈ Pl	λέλυσθε		
3ʳᵈ Pl	λέλυνται		

12.4 PluPerfect Indicative (Optional)

1. The pluperfect tense is a rare tense used to describe an action completed in _____, but felt _____ the action and _____ (or at the time of) the speaker.
2. The middle/passive pluperfect, oddly, has no _____ or _____.
3. The _____ in front of the reduplication is optional.

12.5 PluPerfect Active Indicative (Optional)

1. *Table of Verb Tenses*

Tense	Aug/ Red	Tense stem	TF + CV	Endings	First singular
Present act		pres	o/ε	prim act	λύω
Present mid/pas		pres	o/ε	prim mid/pas	λύομαι
Imperfect act	ε	pres	o/ε	sec act	ἔλυον
Imperfect mid/pas	ε	pres	o/ε	sec mid/pas	ἐλυόμην
Future act		fut act	σ/εσ + o/ε	prim act	λύσω μενῶ
Future mid		fut act	σ/εσ + o/ε	prim mid/pas	πορεύσομαι μενοῦμαι
Future pas		aor pas	θησ/ησ + o/ε	prim mid/pas	λυθήσομαι ἀποσταλήσομαι
Aorist act	ε	aor act	σα/α / o/ε	sec act	ἔλυσα ἔμεινα ἔλαβον
Aorist mid	ε	aor act	σα / o/ε	sec mid/pas	ἐλυσάμην ἐγενόμην
Aorist pas	ε	aor pas	θη/η	sec act	ἐλύθην ἐγράφην
Perfect act	λε		κα/α	prim act	λέλυκα γέγονα
Perfect mid/pas	λε			prim mid/pas	λέλυμαι
Pluperf mid/pas	[ε]λε	perf pas		sec pas	[ε]λελύμην

2. Paradigm of PluPerfect Active Indicative

	First (with TF)	Second (no TF)	Ending
1ˢᵗ Sg			
2ⁿᵈ Sg			
3ʳᵈ Sg			
1ˢᵗ Pl			
2ⁿᵈ Pl			
3ʳᵈ Pl			

12.5 PluPerfect Middle-Passive Indicative (Optional)

1. Table of Verb Tenses

Tense	Aug/Red	Tense stem	TF + CV	Endings	First singular
Present act		pres	o/ε	prim act	λύω
Present mid/pas		pres	o/ε	prim mid/pas	λύομαι
Imperfect act	ε	pres	o/ε	sec act	ἔλυον
Imperfect mid/pas	ε	pres	o/ε	sec mid/pas	ἐλυόμην
Future act		fut act	σ/εσ + o/ε	prim act	λύσω μενῶ
Future mid		fut act	σ/εσ + o/ε	prim mid/pas	πορεύσομαι μενοῦμαι
Future pas		aor pas	θησ/ησ + o/ε	prim mid/pas	λυθήσομαι ἀποσταλήσομαι
Aorist act	ε	aor act	σα/α / o/ε	sec act	ἔλυσα ἔμεινα ἔλαβον
Aorist mid	ε	aor act	σα / o/ε	sec mid/pas	ἐλυσάμην ἐγενόμην
Aorist pas	ε	aor pas	θη/η	sec act	ἐλύθην ἐγράφην

Perfect act	λε	κα/α	prim act	λέλυκα γέγονα
Perfect mid/pas	λε		prim mid/pas	λέλυμαι

2. Paradigm of PluPerfect Middle-Passive Indicative

	Form	Gloss	CV	Ending
1st Sg	(ἐ)λελύμην			
2nd Sg	(ἐ)λελυσο			
3rd Sg	(ἐ)λελυτο			
1st Pl	(ἐ)λελύμεθα			
2nd Pl	(ἐ)λελυσθε			
3rd Pl	(ἐ)λελυντο			

Vocabulary

μηδέ
πρεσβύτερος, α, ον
λίθος, -ου, ὁ
τιοῦτος, -αύτη, -οῦτον

_____ stone
_____ a) and not, nore; b) don't even
_____ 1) older, the older one, elders, ancestors; 2) elders
_____ such, such as this

Parsing

Inflected	Case/Person	Num	Gender/Tense	Voice	Mood	Lexical Form	Gloss
1. λίθοι							
2. μεμαρτύρηκεν							
3. τοιαύτη							
4. πεπίστευκεν							
5. ἀκηκόατε							
6. ἀπέστειλεν							
7. πιστεύετε							
8. πρεσβύτεροι							
9. ἑωράκατε							
10. ἔγνωσαν							
11. θρόνους							
12. πεποίηκεν							
13. βέβληται							
14. εἰσεληλύθατε							
15. ἀπέστειλα							
16. ἐξουσία							
17. ἀναβέβηκεν							
18. ἐβάπτιζεν							
19. ἐβλήθησαν							

Translation

1. καὶ ἀποκριθεὶς εἶπεν, Λέγω ὑμῖν, ἐὰν οὗτοι σιωπήσουσιν, οἱ λίθοι κράξουσιν.[195]

2. καὶ ἀπῆλθεν Μωυσῆς εἰς τὴν παρεμβολήν (camp), αὐτὸς καὶ οἱ πρεσβύτεροι Ισραηλ.[196]

3. Ὅλως (everywhere) ἀκούεται ἐν ὑμῖν πορνεία, καὶ τοιαύτη πορνεία ἥτις οὐδὲ ἐν τοῖς ἔθνεσιν, ὥστε γυναῖκά τινα τοῦ πατρὸς ἔχειν.[197]

4. ὁ πιστεύων εἰς τὸν υἱὸν τοῦ θεοῦ ἔχει τὴν μαρτυρίαν ἐν ἑαυτῷ· ὁ μὴ πιστεύων (one believing) τῷ θεῷ ψεύστην (liar) πεποίηκεν αὐτόν, ὅτι οὐ πεπίστευκεν εἰς τὴν μαρτυρίαν ἣν μεμαρτύρηκεν ὁ θεὸς περὶ τοῦ υἱοῦ αὐτοῦ.[198]

5. καὶ ὁ πέμψας (sent) με πατὴρ ἐκεῖνος μεμαρτύρηκεν περὶ ἐμοῦ. οὔτε φωνὴν αὐτοῦ πώποτε (at any time) ἀκηκόατε οὔτε εἶδος (form) αὐτοῦ ἑωράκατε. καὶ τὸν λόγον αὐτοῦ οὐκ ἔχετε ἐν ὑμῖν μένοντα (abiding), ὅτι ὃν ἀπέστειλεν ἐκεῖνος τούτῳ ὑμεῖς οὐ πιστεύετε. ἐραυνᾶτε (you search) τὰς γραφάς, ὅτι ὑμεῖς δοκεῖτε ἐν αὐταῖς ζωὴν αἰώνιον ἔχειν· καὶ ἐκεῖναί εἰσιν αἱ μαρτυροῦσαι περὶ ἐμοῦ·[199]

---

[195] Lk 19:40.

[196] Num 11:30, LXX.

[197] 1 Cor 5:1. What do you think of the NET and NRSV rendering of the last part of this verse? (Is it, perhaps, a bit more interpretation than necessary?)

[198] 1 Jn 5:10.

[199] Jn 5:37-39.

6. καὶ οἱ εἴκοσι (twenty) τέσσαρες (four) πρεσβύτεροι [οἱ] ἐνώπιον τοῦ θεοῦ
καθήμενοι (who sit) ἐπὶ τοὺς θρόνους αὐτῶν ἔπεσαν (fell) ἐπὶ τὰ πρόσωπα αὐτῶν
καὶ προσεκύνησαν τῷ θεῷ λέγοντες,
Εὐχαριστοῦμέν (we give thanks) σοι, κύριε ὁ θεὸς ὁ παντοκράτωρ,
ὁ ὢν καὶ ὁ ἦν,
ὅτι εἴληφας (you have taken) τὴν δύναμίν σου τὴν μεγάλην
καὶ ἐβασίλευσας.[200]

7. Καὶ ὃς ἂν σκανδαλίσῃ (causes) ἕνα τῶν μικρῶν (little ones) τούτων τῶν
πιστευόντων [εἰς ἐμέ], καλόν ἐστιν αὐτῷ μᾶλλον εἰ περίκειται (placed around)
μύλος (millstone) ὀνικὸς (donkey) περὶ τὸν τράχηλον (neck) αὐτοῦ καὶ βέβληται
εἰς τὴν θάλασσαν.[201]

8. ἐγὼ ἀπέστειλα ὑμᾶς θερίζειν ὃ οὐχ ὑμεῖς κεκοπιάκατε· ἄλλοι κεκοπιάκασιν (have labored) καὶ ὑμεῖς εἰς τὸν κόπον αὐτῶν εἰσεληλύθατε.[202]

9. καὶ οὐδεὶς ἀναβέβηκεν εἰς τὸν οὐρανὸν εἰ μὴ ὁ ἐκ τοῦ οὐρανοῦ καταβάς (descended), ὁ υἱὸς τοῦ ἀνθρώπου.[203]

---

[200] Rev 11:16-17.
[201] Mk 9:42.
[202] Jn 4:38.
[203] Jn 3:13.

13

Subjunctive and Infinitive

13.1 Subjunctive Mood

1. The subjunctive mood is primarily used to _____.
2. As such, the subjunctive mood has no _____ significance.
3. Because of expressing probabilities or possibilities, words in the subjunctive are often used with the words ____ and ____ ("if").
4. Identify the protasis and apodosis in the following sentences:

   a. εἰ δὲ ἐν δακτύλῳ θεοῦ [ἐγὼ] ἐκβάλλω τὰ δαιμόνια (_____), ἄρα ἔφθασεν ἐφ' ὑμᾶς ἡ βασιλεία τοῦ θεοῦ (_____).[204]

   b. εἰ δὲ ὑμεῖς Χριστοῦ (_____), ἄρα τοῦ Ἀβραὰμ σπέρμα ἐστέ, κατ' ἐπαγγελίαν κληρονόμοι (_____).[205]

   c. καὶ εἶπεν αὐτῷ, Ταῦτά σοι πάντα δώσω (_____) ἐὰν πεσὼν προσκυνήσῃς μοι (_____).[206]

---

[204] Lk 11:20. Cf. Mt 12:28.
[205] Gal 3:29.
[206] Mt 4:9.

d. εἰ δὲ Χριστὸς οὐκ ἐγήγερται (_____), κενὸν ἄρα καὶ τὸ κήρυγμα ἡμῶν (_____), κενὴ καὶ ἡ πίστις ὑμῶν…[207]

13.2-3 Present and Aorist Subjunctive

1. The present subjunctive indicates a _____ probability or possibility, while the aorist subjunctive indicates a _____ probability or possibility.

Table of Subjunctive Verb Tenses

Tense	Tense stem	TF + CV	Endings	First singular

---

[207] 1 Cor 15:14.

Table of εἰμί Verbs (Complete)

	Imperfect	Present	Future	Subjunctive
1 sg				
2 sg				
3 sg				
1 pl				
2 pl				
3 pl				

13.4 Infinitive

1. The infinitive is indeclinable, which means it uses the declension endings. True or False
2. The English word "to" must *always* be supplied in translating the infinitive. True or False
3. The infinitive does not have person or number. True or False
4. Fill out the Table of Infinitive Tenses:

Tense	Ending

Vocabulary

δίκαιος, -α, -ον _____
ἀπολύω _____
ἀπόλλυμι _____
εἴτε _____
μέλλω _____

_____ upright, just
_____ a) be in the offing, be about (to), being going (to), (in the) future, to come; b) have in mind, intend, plan (on), to delay
_____ 1) destroy, ruin, kill, destroy; 2) lose, perish
_____ 1) release, deliver, free; 2) send off, dismiss; 4) go off, leave
_____ If…(or) if, whether…or

Parsing

Inflected	Case/Person	Num	Gender/Tense	Voice	Mood	Lexical Form	Gloss
1. ἐξερχώμεθα							
2. εἴπῃ							
3. ἀπολύσω							
4. δοξάζηται							
5. ἁγίου							
6. Ἐγένετο							
7. ἤμελλεν							
8. σχῶ							
9. θεωρῆσαι							
10. παρακαλεῖν							
11. ἀποστείλῃ							
12. εἴπω							
13. ἄγειν							
14. δίκαιά							
15. γενηθῶμεν							
16. ἐρωτήσω							
17. φαγεῖν							
18. σχῶμεν							
19. ἠσπάζοντο							
20. εἴπωμεν							

Translation

1. ἐξερχώμεθα πρὸς αὐτόν...[208] _____

2. ἐγὼ δὲ λέγω ὑμῖν ὅτι πᾶς ὁ ὀργιζόμενος (is angry) τῷ ἀδελφῷ αὐτοῦ ἔνοχος (liable) ἔσται τῇ κρίσει (court)· ὃς δ' ἂν εἴπῃ τῷ ἀδελφῷ αὐτοῦ, Ῥακά, ἔνοχος ἔσται τῷ συνεδρίῳ (court)· ὃς δ' ἂν εἴπῃ, Μωρέ, ἔνοχος ἔσται εἰς τὴν γέενναν τοῦ πυρός.[209]

3. Καὶ ἰδοὺ εἷς προσελθὼν αὐτῷ εἶπεν, Διδάσκαλε, τί ἀγαθὸν ποιήσω ἵνα σχῶ ζωὴν αἰώνιον;[210]

4. Ἐγερθείς (Get up!) παράλαβε (take!) τὸ παιδίον καὶ τὴν μητέρα αὐτοῦ καὶ φεῦγε (flee) εἰς Αἴγυπτον (Egypt) καὶ ἴσθι (be!) ἐκεῖ ἕως ἂν εἴπω σοι.[211]

5. Καὶ νῦν, τεκνία, μένετε ἐν αὐτῷ, ἵνα ἐὰν φανερωθῇ σχῶμεν παρρησίαν (confidence) καὶ μὴ αἰσχυνθῶμεν (be disgraced) ἀπ' αὐτοῦ ἐν τῇ παρουσίᾳ αὐτοῦ.[212]

---

[208] Heb 13:10.
[209] Mt 5:22.
[210] Mt 19:16.
[211] Mt 2:13.
[212] 1 Jn 2:28.

6. λέγοντες, Εἰ σὺ εἶ ὁ Χριστός, εἰπὸν (tell!) ἡμῖν. εἶπεν δὲ αὐτοῖς, Ἐὰν ὑμῖν εἴπω, οὐ μὴ πιστεύσητε· ἐὰν δὲ ἐρωτήσω, οὐ μὴ ἀποκριθῆτε.[213]

7. ἐὰν εἴπωμεν ὅτι ἁμαρτίαν οὐκ ἔχομεν, ἑαυτοὺς πλανῶμεν (we deceive) καὶ ἡ ἀλήθεια οὐκ ἔστιν ἐν ἡμῖν.[214]

8. Τὸ λοιπὸν (finally) προσεύχεσθε, ἀδελφοί, περὶ ἡμῶν, ἵνα ὁ λόγος τοῦ κυρίου τρέχῃ (will speed ahead) καὶ δοξάζηται καθὼς καὶ πρὸς ὑμᾶς.[215]

9. ἔσται γὰρ μέγας ἐνώπιον τοῦ κυρίου, καὶ οἶνον καὶ σίκερα οὐ μὴ πίῃ, καὶ πνεύματος ἁγίου πλησθήσεται ἔτι ἐκ κοιλίας (womb) μητρὸς αὐτοῦ, καὶ πολλοὺς τῶν υἱῶν Ἰσραὴλ ἐπιστρέψει (he will turn) ἐπὶ κύριον τὸν θεὸν αὐτῶν.[216]

---

[213] Lk 22:67-68.
[214] 1 Jn 1:8.
[215] 2 Thess 3:1.
[216] Lk 1:15-16.

10. Κατὰ δὲ ἑορτὴν (feast) εἰώθει (was accustomed) ὁ ἡγεμὼν (governor) ἀπολύειν ἕνα τῷ ὄχλῳ δέσμιον (prisoner) ὃν ἤθελον. εἶχον δὲ τότε δέσμιον ἐπίσημον (well-known) λεγόμενον Βαραββᾶν. συνηγμένων (gathered together) οὖν αὐτῶν εἶπεν αὐτοῖς ὁ Πιλᾶτος, Τίνα θέλετε ἀπολύσω ὑμῖν, Ἰησοῦν τὸν Βαραββᾶν ἢ Ἰησοῦν τὸν λεγόμενον (the one called) Χριστόν;[217]

11. Μετὰ δὲ ταῦτα ἀνέδειξεν (appointed) ὁ κύριος ἑτέρους ἑβδομήκοντα (seventy) [δύο], καὶ ἀπέστειλεν αὐτοὺς ἀνὰ δύο [δύο] πρὸ προσώπου αὐτοῦ εἰς πᾶσαν πόλιν καὶ τόπον οὗ ἤμελλεν αὐτὸς ἔρχεσθαι.[218]

12. ...ἵνα δυνατὸς ᾖ καὶ παρακαλεῖν ἐν τῇ διδασκαλίᾳ τῇ ὑγιαινούσῃ (sound) καὶ τοὺς ἀντιλέγοντας (those who contract) ἐλέγχειν (to refute).[219]

---

[217] Mt 27:15-17.
[218] Lk 10:1.
[219] Tit 1:9.

13. καὶ ἐπηρώτα (he as asking) αὐτόν, Τί ὄνομά σοι; καὶ λέγει αὐτῷ, Λεγιὼν ὄνομά μοι, ὅτι πολλοί ἐσμεν. καὶ παρεκάλει αὐτὸν πολλὰ ἵνα μὴ αὐτὰ ἀποστείλῃ ἔξω τῆς χώρας (country).[220]

14. οὐκ ἐξ ἔργων τῶν ἐν δικαιοσύνῃ ἃ ἐποιήσαμεν ἡμεῖς ἀλλὰ κατὰ τὸ αὐτοῦ ἔλεος (mercy) ἔσωσεν ἡμᾶς διὰ λουτροῦ (washing) παλιγγενεσίας (regeneration) καὶ ἀνακαινώσεως (renewing) πνεύματος ἁγίου, οὗ ἐξέχεεν (he poured out) ἐφ' ἡμᾶς πλουσίως (richly) διὰ Ἰησοῦ Χριστοῦ τοῦ σωτῆρος ἡμῶν, ἵνα δικαιωθέντες (being justified) τῇ ἐκείνου χάριτι κληρονόμοι (heirs) γενηθῶμεν κατ' ἐλπίδα ζωῆς αἰωνίου.[221]

---

[220] Mk 5:9-10.
[221] Tit 3:5-7.

14

Imperative and -μι Verbs

14.1 Imperative

1. The imperative mood makes an assertion or asks a question. True or False
2. The imperative has no time significance. True or False
3. Fill out the Table of Imperative Morphemes:

	All Active and Aorist Passive	Middle/Passive
2ⁿᵈ Sg		
3ʳᵈ Sg		
2ⁿᵈ Pl		
3ʳᵈ Pl		

14.2 -μι Verbs

1. -μι verbs end in -μι instead of:
   a. ο/ω
   b. a consonant
   c. ε
2. -μι verbs undergo reduplication like the perfect tense, but instead of being separated by an ε, they are separated by an ι. True or False
3. -μι verbs use the tense formative ka in the perfect (as usual), but also in the aorist tense. True or False
4. Fill out the Table of Active Indicative -μι Verbs:

	Present	Imperfect	Future	Aorist	Perfect
1st Sg					
2nd Sg					
3rd Sg					
1st Pl					
2nd Pl					
3rd Pl					

Vocabulary

ἀνίστημι _____
δίδωμι _____
ἔθνος, -ους, τό _____
λοιπός, -ή, -όν _____
Μωϋσῆς, -έως, ὁ _____
παραδίδωμι _____
πίπτω _____
ὑπάρχω _____

_____ 1) remaining; 2) other, rest (of); 3) from now on, henceforth, at last, from now on, in the future, otherwise, furthermore, finally
_____ Moses
_____ hand over
_____ a) fall, collapse, fall; b) fall (down); c) fall/perish; d) fall
_____ 1) be there, take place, have place, be at (one's disposal, belong (to), property, holdings; 2) be
_____ 1) raise up; b) rise (up), get up
_____ give
_____ 1) people (group); 2) non-Israelite persons, Gentiles

Parsing

	Inflected	Case/Person	Num	Gender/Tense	Voice	Mood	Lexical Form	Gloss
1.	ἀπολέσωσιν							
2.	πεσεῖται[222]							
3.	δικαίους							
4.	ἀπολῦσαί							
5.	Μέλλει							
6.	παρεδόθη							
7.	ὑπάρχειν							
8.	Λάβετε							
9.	γέγραπται							
10.	ποιείτω							
11.	βαπτισθῆναι							
12.	ἀπολέσαι							
13.	ποιήσωμεν							
14.	ἐπερωτάτωσαν							
15.	προφήτης							

1. ἠγάγετε γὰρ τοὺς ἄνδρας τούτους οὔτε ἱεροσύλους (temple robbers) οὔτε βλασφημοῦντας (blasphemers) τὴν θεὸν ἡμῶν.[223]

2. Καὶ ἐσθιόντων αὐτῶν λαβὼν ἄρτον εὐλογήσας ἔκλασεν (broke) καὶ ἔδωκεν αὐτοῖς καὶ εἶπεν, Λάβετε, τοῦτό ἐστιν τὸ σῶμά μου.[224]

---

[222] This form exhibits a significant stem change of one of this chapter's vocabulary words.
[223] Acts 19:37. Note the gender of τὴν.
[224] Mk 14:22.

3. ἀποκριθεὶς δὲ ἔλεγεν αὐτοῖς, Ὁ ἔχων δύο χιτῶνας (coats) μεταδότω τῷ μὴ ἔχοντι, καὶ ὁ ἔχων βρώματα (food) ὁμοίως (likewise) ποιείτω.[225]

4. Πάντα μοι παρεδόθη ὑπὸ τοῦ πατρός μου, καὶ οὐδεὶς ἐπιγινώσκει τὸν υἱὸν εἰ μὴ ὁ πατήρ, οὐδὲ τὸν πατέρα τις ἐπιγινώσκει εἰ μὴ ὁ υἱὸς καὶ ᾧ ἐὰν βούληται ὁ υἱὸς ἀποκαλύψαι.[226]

5. καὶ ἐξελθόντες οἱ Φαρισαῖοι εὐθὺς μετὰ τῶν Ἡρῳδιανῶν συμβούλιον ἐδίδουν κατ' αὐτοῦ ὅπως αὐτὸν ἀπολέσωσιν.[227]

6. Καὶ ἦν διδάσκων τὸ καθ' ἡμέραν ἐν τῷ ἱερῷ. οἱ δὲ ἀρχιερεῖς καὶ οἱ γραμματεῖς ἐζήτουν αὐτὸν ἀπολέσαι καὶ οἱ πρῶτοι τοῦ λαοῦ,[228]

7. πορευθέντες δὲ μάθετε τί ἐστιν, Ἔλεος θέλω καὶ οὐ θυσίαν· οὐ γὰρ ἦλθον καλέσαι δικαίους ἀλλὰ ἁμαρτωλούς.[229]

---

[225] Lk 3:11.
[226] Mt 11:27.
[227] Mk 3:6.
[228] Lk 19:47.
[229] Mt 9:13.

8. λέγει οὖν αὐτῷ ὁ Πιλᾶτος, Ἐμοὶ οὐ λαλεῖς; οὐκ οἶδας ὅτι ἐξουσίαν ἔχω ἀπολῦσαί σε καὶ ἐξουσίαν ἔχω σταυρῶσαί (to crucify) σε;[230]

9. Συστρεφομένων (were gathering) δὲ αὐτῶν ἐν τῇ Γαλιλαίᾳ εἶπεν αὐτοῖς ὁ Ἰησοῦς, Μέλλει ὁ υἱὸς τοῦ ἀνθρώπου παραδίδοσθαι εἰς χεῖρας ἀνθρώπων,[231]

10. οὐχὶ δύο στρουθία (sparrows) ἀσσαρίου (penny) πωλεῖται (sell); καὶ ἓν ἐξ αὐτῶν οὐ πεσεῖται ἐπὶ τὴν γῆν ἄνευ (apart from) τοῦ πατρὸς ὑμῶν.[232]

---

[230] John 19:10.
[231] Mt 17:23.
[232] Mt 10:29.